Great American Cookout

Great American Cookout

Gregg R. Gillespie

Black Dog
& Leventhal
Publishers

Published by
Black Dog & Leventhal Publishers, Inc.
151 West 19th Street
New York, NY 10011

Distributed by
Workman Publishing Company
708 Broadway
New York, NY 10003

Cover and interior design by 27.12 Design, Ltd.
Additional text by Benjamin Ikenson

Printed and bound in China

ISBN: 1-57912-235-3

h g f e d c b

Library of Congress Cataloging-in-Publication Data

Gillespie, Gregg R., 1934-
Great American Cookout: 250 down-home dishes that taste great outdoors / by Gregg R. Gillespie
p. cm.

ISBN 1-57912-235-3

1. Outdoor cookery. 2. Menus. I. Title
TX823 .G495 2002 641.5'78--dc21 2001008074

Great American Cookout Cookbook

Small Bites & Big Platters

★

Fourth of July Bash

SIPS AND STARTERS

•

Bloody Marys
Honey Lemonade
Deviled Eggs
Fresh Garden Dip

SALADS

•

Fresh Tomato Salad
European Green Salad

ENTREES

•

The Perfect Burger
Grilled Vegetables

SIDES

•

Grilled Corn on the Cob

FROM THE BAKERY

•

Apple Cobbler
Buttermilk Biscuits

Savory Stuffed Mushrooms

About 24 servings

2 pounds fresh mushrooms, washed and stemmed

1 (8 ounce) bottle Italian salad dressing

1/4 cup sour cream

1 (3 ounce) package cream cheese, at room temperature

1/4 cup crumbled cheese, like feta or goat

1 tablespoon chopped green onion

2 tablespoons hot or mild chili sauce

1 tablespoon fresh lemon juice

1/2 teaspoon Worcestershire sauce

1 (4-1/4 ounce) can shrimp, drained, well rinsed,
   and finely chopped

Grated Parmesan Cheese, for garnish

1. *Place the mushrooms in a bowl, drizzle with the dressing, cover tightly, and refrigerate for at least 4 hours.*

2. *In a second bowl, stir together the sour cream, cream cheese, cheese, green onion, chili sauce, lemon juice, Worcestershire sauce, and shrimp. Cover with plastic wrap, and refrigerate until needed.*

3. *Set aside the mushrooms on a paper towel, stem side down, to drain.*

4. *Fill each mushroom with the cheese mixture, garnish with the Parmesan, and serve at once, or re-cover and refrigerate until needed.*

For a lighter dish, substitute lowfat or nonfat sour cream for the full-fat version.

Sausage Pockets

8 servings

Oil or shortening, for greasing the pan

1 tablespoon cornmeal

3/4 pound Italian sausage, casings removed

1 clove garlic, minced

1/4 cup chopped shallots

1 cup chopped fresh spinach

3/4 cup shredded mozzarella cheese

1/4 cup chopped fresh mushrooms

2 tablespoons grated Parmesan cheese

2 (8 ounce) packages refrigerated dinner crescent rolls

1 large egg

1 tablespoon water

1. *Position the rack in the center of the oven and preheat to 350° F. Lightly grease a baking sheet and sprinkle it with cornmeal.*

2. *In a saucepan, cook the sausage over medium heat, stirring with a fork, for 7 or 8 minutes or until browned. Add the garlic, shallots, and spinach and cook for about 5 minutes longer, or until tender. Add the mozzarella, mushrooms, and Parmesan and stir until the cheeses begin to melt. Remove from the heat.*

3. *Position the rolls into 8 rectangles and smooth along the perforations to seal. Spread about 1/2 cup of the sausage mixture on one half of each rectangle, leaving a 1/2-inch border.*

4. *In a small bowl, whisk the egg and water until foamy. Using a pastry brush, brush the borders and top of each rectangle and fold the empty half over the filling, pressing to secure. Transfer to the baking sheet and bake for 15 to 20 minutes or until golden brown. Cool slightly on wire racks and serve warm.*

Baked Olive Bundles

24 servings

Oil or shortening, for greasing the pan

1 cup grated mozzarella cheese

1 small can tomato purée

2 tablespoons butter or margarine, at room temperature

1/2 cup flour

24 pimiento-stuffed olives, drained and patted dry

1. *Position a rack in the center of the oven and preheat to 400° F. Lightly grease a baking or cookie sheet.*

2. *In a bowl, blend together the cheese, tomato purée, and butter. Blend in the flour, a little at a time, to form a sticky dough.*

3. *Drop by tablespoons onto the prepared baking sheet, and press into patties. Press the olives into the centers, and pull the dough up to cover completely. Bake for about 15 minutes, or until golden brown. Remove from the oven and serve.*

For olive bundles with more bite, red pepper cheese can be substituted for the mozzarella.

Deviled Eggs

About 32 servings

16 hard-boiled eggs, shelled
1 cup mayonnaise
4 teaspoons cider vinegar
4 teaspoons onion powder
1 teaspoon dry mustard, or to taste
Salt and pepper, to taste
Paprika, or edible blossoms, for garnish

1. *Using a sharp wet knife, cut the eggs in half. Remove the yolks and place in a bowl.*
2. *To the bowl, add the mayonnaise, vinegar, onion powder, mustard, and salt and pepper to taste. Using a spoon or pastry bag fitted with a star tip, press the mixture into the indentation in the egg whites. Sprinkle with paprika, or garnish with blossoms, and serve immediately.*

Those Devilish Deviled Eggs

In culinary lingo, the word "deviled" usually refers to the preparation of food, often chopped and spiked with spicy seasonings. Recipe variations on the deviled egg run a wide gamut, but there is typically one thing common to all: the delicacies are always dynamite at a party, as small morsels packing huge and sumptuous explosions of flavor. Deviled eggs truly do tempt: set them out on your table, and watch the feasters flock. So many find them impossible to resist, it's likely these diabolically delicious treats will be named the eighth mortal sin.

Crunchy Cucumber Rounds

About 48 servings

1 cup diced unpeeled green apple

1/2 cup canned crushed pineapple, well drained

1/4 cup finely chopped pecans or walnuts

1/4 cup sour cream

Salt, to taste

3 medium cucumbers, chilled

Fresh parsley, snipped, for garnish

1. *In a bowl, combine the apple, pineapple, pecans, sour cream, and salt. Cover and refrigerate for at least 1 hour.*
2. *Score the cucumbers by drawing the tines of a fork lengthwise down the rind. Cut into 1/4-inch thick slices, place on paper towels, and pat dry.*
3. *Spoon about a teaspoon of the fruit mixture onto each cucumber slice, garnish with the parsley, and serve immediately, or cover and refrigerate for up to 2 hours.*

Cucumber Rafts

About 10 to 12 servings

3/4 cup finely chopped cooked chicken

1/3 cup finely chopped celery

2 tablespoons chopped pimiento

2 tablespoons mayonnaise

Salt and pepper, to taste

1 medium cucumber, trimmed

Finely chopped peanuts, for garnish

1. *In a bowl, blend together the chicken, celery, pimiento, mayonnaise, and salt and pepper. Cover and refrigerate for 2 hours.*
2. *Using a sharp knife, cut the cucumber into 1/4-inch thick slices. Place in a bowl, cover, and refrigerate until ready.*
3. *To assemble, drop a spoonful of the chicken mixture into the center of each slice of cucumber, arrange on a platter, sprinkle with nuts, and serve at once, or chill until needed.*

For a more piquant flavor, substitute pickle relish for the celery.

Spinach-Feta Triangles

About 24 appetizers

1/2 cup vegetable oil

2 large onions, chopped

2 (10 ounce) packages frozen chopped spinach, thawed, drained,
    and squeezed

2 tablespoons snipped fresh dill

2 tablespoons flour

8 ounces feta cheese, crumbled

4 eggs, lightly beaten

Salt and pepper, to taste

2 packages frozen puff pastry, thawed

2 egg yolks, beaten with 2 teaspoons water

1. *Preheat oven to 375° F.*
2. *Place oil in a large saucepan over medium heat, add the onions and sauté until soft. Stir in the spinach, dill, and flour and ocook for about 10 minutes, or until most of the moisture has evaporated. Remove from the heat and mix in the cheese, eggs, and salt and pepper.*
3. *Cut the pastry into twenty-four 3-inch squares and place a heaping tablespoon of the spinach-feta mixture in the center of each. Moisten edges of the pastry with water and fold to create triangles, then press the edges together firmly with a fork to seal. Lightly brush the pastries with the egg wash.*
4. *Place in the oven and bake for about 20 minutes, or until golden.*

Salmon Croquettes

4 servings

1 (14-3/4 ounce) can salmon

1 cup breadcrumbs

1 large egg, beaten

2 tablespoons snipped chives

Salt and pepper, to taste

1 tablespoon canola oil

Dill Dipping Sauce (see page 135), for serving

1. *In a bowl, combine the salmon, breadcrumbs, egg, chives, and salt and pepper to taste. Form into 4 patties.*
2. *Heat the oil in a skillet and sauté the patties for about 10 minutes or until both sides are a light golden brown. Remove from the heat and serve immediately with Dill Dipping Sauce on the side.*

Thai Turkey Nibbles

About 25 to 30 servings

Oil or shortening, for greasing the pan

1 pound ground turkey

1/4 cup chopped green onion

1 teaspoon chili powder

1/4 teaspoon black pepper

2 tablespoons soy sauce

1/2 teaspoon sesame oil

1 medium cucumber

Thai Relish (see page 135), for serving

1. *Position a rack in the center of the oven and preheat to 350° F. Lightly grease a 13- x 9- x 2-inch baking pan.*
2. *In a bowl, combine the turkey, green onion, chili powder, black pepper, soy sauce, and sesame oil. Pinch off pieces and form into small balls about the size of walnuts. Place the balls in the prepared baking pan.*
3. *Bake for about 15 to 20 minutes, turning, until the meatballs are light brown. Remove from the oven and transfer to a serving plate.*
4. *Using a sharp knife, cut the cucumbers in half lengthwise, cut the halves into 1/4-inch thick slices, and arrange around plate. Serve meatballs with Thai Relish on the side.*

Tortilla Bites

About 72 servings

1 (8 ounce) package cream cheese, at room temperature
1 (4 ounce) can chopped green chiles, drained
1 (4 ounce) jar chopped pimiento, drained
1/2 cup chopped ripe olives
12 (6 inch) flour tortillas
Jarred mild salsa, as dipping sauce

1. *In a bowl, blend together cream cheese, chiles, pimiento, and olives. Spread 1 heaping tablespoonful of the mixture evenly on each tortilla, roll up pencil tight, and place seam side down on a cookie sheet. Cover, and refrigerate for at least 2 hours.*
2. *When ready, use a sharp serrated knife to cut each roll into 1-inch pieces. Arrange the pieces on a serving platter with the salsa in a bowl on the side.*

To spice up the flavors and colors of this dish, the flour tortillas can be replaced by jalapeño, spinach, or tomato varieties.

Snack Scramble

About 8 quarts

1 (12 ounce) package Wheat Chex
1 (10 ounce) package Cheerios
1 (6-1/2 ounce) package Rice Chex
1 (6-1/2 ounce) package pretzel sticks
1 (6-1/2 ounce) package pretzel nuggets
2 cups salad oil
2 tablespoons Worcestershire sauce
1 tablespoon garlic powder
1 tablespoon seasoned salt

1. *Position a rack in the center of the oven and preheat to 250° F.*
2. *In a saucepan, soup kettle, or Dutch oven, combine the Wheat Chex, Cheerios, Rice Chex, and pretzels.*
3. *In a bowl, stir together oil, Worcestershire sauce, garlic powder, and seasoned salt. Drizzle over the cereal mixture, toss to coat, and bake on a non-stick or greased cookie sheet, stirring frequently, for about 1-1/2 to 2 hours. Remove from the oven and store in an airtight container until needed.*

Flaunt That Flag

Decorating for Independence Day? Three words—red, white, and blue—that's all you need to remember. The colors will do the rest. Deck your pad with as many patriotic accessories as your home can handle. Here are a few tips before the fireworks fill the skies.

- *Alternate between red-and-white and blue-and-white checked tablecloths.*
- *Plant small flags in tiny moss-topped pots and place in front of each seat.*
- *Thread red, white, and blue streamers through openwork in porch and through the yard.*
- *Bake Great Aunt Ida's Easy Yellow Cake and decorate it with American flag-inspired Rich Buttercream Frosting (see page 206).*
- *Use a combination of red, white, and blue plastic cups and flatware. It's festive and makes cleanup simple.*
- *Adorn the walls with portraits of the founding fathers—or try to find some of those old "Uncle Sam Wants You" posters—and slap red, white, and blue ribbons on them.*
- *Place bouquets of red, white, and blue flowers— red and white tulips or roses, blue forget-me-nots, and daisies—on tables or poolside.*

Gazpacho

About 4 servings

2 cloves garlic, peeled

6 large ripe tomatoes, peeled (see Box on page 66)

1 large onion, peeled and coarsely chopped

1 green bell pepper, stemmed, cored, seeded,
    and coarsely chopped

2 small cucumbers, peeled, seeded, and coarsely chopped

1/2 cup canola oil

1/2 cup fresh lemon juice

3 cups tomato juice, chilled

Salt and cayenne pepper, to taste

Snipped fresh chives, for garnish (optional)

1. *Place the tomatoes and garlic in a blender and process on high until smooth. Add 1/4 of the green pepper, 1/4 of the onion, and 1/2 of the cucumber and process until puréed but slightly chunky. Place in the refrigerator and chill.*
2. *Chop the remaining vegetables and place them in separate serving dishes in the refrigerator.*
3. *Just before serving, whisk together the canola oil, lemon juice, tomato juice, salt, and cayenne pepper. Add to the puréed vegetables. Ladle into soup bowls and garnish with chives, if desired. Pass the chopped vegetables at table, if you wish.*

Chilled Cucumber Soup

4 to 6 servings

2 potatoes, peeled and diced

1 cup chicken stock

1 cup dry white wine

2 cucumbers, peeled and coarsely grated

4 celery stalks, trimmed and coarsely grated

1 teaspoon grated onion

1 cup heavy cream

1 teaspoon salt

Pepper, to taste

Cook the potatoes and the onion in the stock and wine at a slow boil, uncovered, for about 15 minutes. Cover and continue cooking until tender. Remove from heat, and let stand, covered, for about 10 minutes. Purée the potatoes and cooking liquid in a food mill or food processor. Stir in the cucumber, celery, onion, heavy cream, salt, and pepper. Chill until ready to be served.

Nachos Olé

About 24 servings

1 cup refried beans
24 round tortilla chips
1/4 cup mild salsa
1/2 cup shredded Monterey Jack cheese
24 black olive slices

1. *Position the broiler rack about 5 inches from the heat source and preheat the broiler.*
2. *Arrange the tortilla chips on a cookie sheet. Evenly spread 1 heaping teaspoon of the beans on each chip, top with 1/2 teaspoon salsa, 1 teaspoon cheese, and 1 olive slice.*
3. *Place in the broiler and cook for about 2 to 3 minutes, or until the cheese melts. The nachos are best served immediately.*

Nacho Toppers

Because tortilla chips are relatively basic in flavor, they can be topped by any number of ingredients to make a fun and tasty treat: black beans; pinto beans; salsa; sour cream; melted cheddar cheese; black olives; green olives; avocado slices; jalapeños; grilled onions; green or red peppers; cilantro; strips of grilled chicken or steak; grilled shrimp; crispy bacon; the list goes on and on. Did you leave a bit of last night's hamburger in the fridge? Toss it into the mix. Or try a new age slant on the snack with shaved carrots, asparagus spears, broccoli, and marinated tofu cubes.

An American Tune

Music is one of our nation's wealthiest and most influential cultural assets—so let the fireworks begin! If you're planning a particulary patriotic ambiance for your next shindig—say, for example, an all-day July 4th Bash—turn to the rich legacy of American music.

For a down-home, woodsy feel, try some classic country or Southern rock. For swanky sophistication, throw on some jazz or blues records. To strike a stronger chord, play some boogie-woogie, surf rock, or classic rock. Here's a list of suggestions to get you grooving:

ROCK AND ROLL:
Bruce Springsteen, John Mellencamp, Lenny Kravitz, Neil Young, Lynryd Skynyrd, The Allman Brothers, The Band, The Beach Boys, Don McLean, The Grateful Dead, Creedence Clearwater Revival

COUNTRY:
Hank Williams, Johnny Cash, Patsy Cline, Willie Nelson, Garth Brooks, The Dixie Chicks, Tim McGraw, Brooks and Dunn, George Strait

OLDIES BUT GOODIES:
Chuck Berry, Carl Perkins, Elvis Presley, Little Richard, Fats Domino, The Temptations, The Supremes, Smokey Robinson, Buddy Holly, The Everly Brothers

JAZZ & BLUES:
Count Basie, Benny Goodman, Glenn Miller, Duke Ellington, Miles Davis, John Coltrane, Ella Fitzgerald, Billie Holliday, Dave Brubeck, Louis Armstrong, B.B. King, John Lee Hooker, Stevie Ray Vaughn, Buddy Guy

FOLK SINGER/SONGWRITER:
Joan Baez, Woody Guthrie, Bob Dylan, The Kingston Trio, Joni Mitchell, James Taylor, Pete Seeger

Sesame Chicken Platter

About 8 servings

2 whole skinless, boneless chicken breasts
1 egg
1/3 cup water
1/3 cup all-purpose flour
2 teaspoons sesame seeds
Salt and pepper, to taste
Red onion, sliced into rings, for garnish
Great American Sweet and Sour Sauce (see page 127), for serving

1. *Thoroughly wash the chicken under running water and pat dry using paper towels. Using a sharp knife, cut into 1-inch dice.*
2. *In a skillet, saucepan, or deep fryer, heat about 2 to 3 inches of oil to 375° F.*
3. *Meanwhile, in a bowl, beat together the egg and water until blended. Beat in the flour, sesame seeds, and salt and pepper until smooth.*
4. *Using a fork or wooden skewer, working a few pieces at a time, dip the chicken pieces in the batter, and then gently into the hot oil. Cook for about 2 minutes per side, turning, until a golden brown color. Transfer to a wire rack covered with paper towels and drain. Repeat until all the chicken pieces are cooked.*
5. *Place the Sweet and Sour Sauce in the center of a platter, arrange the chicken pieces and sliced onion around the edge, and serve.*

Egg Salad Tea Sandwiches

10 servings

1 cup small curd cottage cheese
2 hard-boiled eggs, shelled and coarsely chopped
1 to 2 tablespoons thinly sliced green onion
1 tablespoon chopped red bell pepper
1 tablespoon chopped black olives
1 teaspoon mustard
10 slices round cocktail rye bread or other dense bread
Watercress sprigs, rinsed and patted dry, for garnish

1. In a bowl combine the cottage cheese, eggs, green onion, bell peppers, olives, and mustard, and mix until just incorporated (eggs should remain chunky). Cover with plastic wrap and refrigerate for at least 2 hours.
2. When ready, spread the mixture evenly over the slices of the bread, garnish with the watercress, and serve.

Cookie cutters can be used to cut full-sized bread slices into interesting shapes.

Cucumber & Radish Tea Sandwiches

About 32 servings

1 loaf thinly sliced dense white bread

1 (8 ounce) tub whipped cream cheese

1/4 cup snipped fresh dill

1 large cucumber, rinsed and sliced paper thin

16 radishes, trimmed and sliced paper thin

Salt and pepper, to taste

Fresh dill, for garnish

1. Cut the bread slices in half diagonally.
2. In a bowl, combine the cream cheese and spipped dill.
3. Spread each bread slice with the dill cream cheese. Top half of the slices with the cucumber, and half with the radish. Season with salt and pepper to taste, garnish with the fresh dill, and serve.

Roast Beef & Horseradish Cream Sandwiches

About 8 servings

1 (8 ounce) package cream cheese, at room temperature

2 to 3 tablespoons horseradish

2 tablespoons snipped fresh parsley or cilantro

Salt to taste

16 slices roast beef

16 slices Swiss cheese

4 large slices dark rye bread, halved

2 medium tomatoes, thinly sliced

2 small zucchini, thinly sliced

1. In a bowl, using an electric mixer, blend together the cream cheese, horseradish, parsley, and salt until smooth. Cover and refrigerate for at least 2 hours.
2. When ready, transfer the cream cheese mixture into a decorative glass bowl, and place in the center of a large round serving platter. Roll the roast beef into tight, pencil-size rolls and arrange around the bowl. Between the meat rolls arrange the cheese, bread, tomato, and zucchini and serve.

Charm with Cheese

Ever notice the conglomeration of people huddled near a specific table at a party, exchanging pleasantries amongst themselves, but looking somewhat conspiratorial? They're there to ravage the cheese platter, which is a surefire hit on almost any occasion.

An ornate cheese platter can make for either a great starter or a fine finale to an elegant meal with a larger crowd. Tastes differ, so variety is crucial: some mild, some sharp, some smooth, some soft. Stop at a gourmet grocer and consider Gorgonzola, Roquefort, Edam or Gouda, Manchego, cheddar, brick, Stilton, Swiss, Camembert, Chevre (goat cheese), Trappist, Gjetost, Liederkranz, and Bel Paese. Arrange cheeses on a wooden tray or a large platter, and if you're nibbling outdoors, be sure to place it in the shade. Add crisp crackers of several sizes and kinds. Fruit and cheese are excellent companions, so keep a bowl of fresh fruit or a dish of cut fruit nearby. If anyone on your guest list is lactose-intolerant, there are plenty of non-dairy cheeses made with soy available on the market.

Fresh Tomato Bruschetta

36 servings

1 (22 inch) baguette, cut into 36 slices

1/4 cup plus 1 tablespoon extra virgin olive oil

4 large ripe tomatoes (2 red, 2 yellow) stemmed, seeded, and diced

2 cloves garlic, minced

Salt and pepper, to taste

Chopped fresh basil, for garnish

1. *Preheat the grill or broiler.*
2. *Brush the bread slices with 1/4 cup of the olive oil and grill until lightly toasted.*
3. *Combine the remaining ingredients in a bowl with the remaining olive oil and spoon on top of the bread slices. Garnish with the basil and serve.*

Chicken Hero with Crispy Bacon

4 to 6 servings

1 (16 inch) loaf French, Italian, or sourdough bread

2 tablespoons butter or margarine, at room temperature

4 slices cooked bacon, crumbled

6 ounces thinly sliced Swiss or mild cheddar cheese

4 fresh lettuce leaves, washed and patted dry

1/4 cup Horseradish-Mustard Spread (see page 126)

6 ounces cooked chicken breasts, thinly sliced

4 thin slices red onion, in rings

1. *Using a sharp knife, cut the bread in half lengthwise and lay both halves on a flat surface with the cut sides up. Spread each half with the butter, then layer the bacon, cheese, and lettuce on the bottom half. Drizzle the Horseradish-Mustard Spread over the top, and finish with a layer of chicken and onion. Replace the top half of the bread, and use a sharp knife to cut into small slices.*
2. *Arrange on a platter and serve immediately, or cover lightly with plastic wrap and chill until needed.*

Chicken Vegetable Pizza

About 8 appetizer servings

Oil or shortening, for greasing the pan
1 (8 ounce) package refrigerated crescent dinner rolls
1 cup diced cooked chicken
1 large yellow onion, peeled and sliced into thin rings
1 large green bell pepper, stemmed, seeded, and sliced into rings
1/2 pound fresh mushrooms, washed and sliced
1/2 cup sliced olives
1 (10-1/2 ounce) can pizza sauce with cheese
1 teaspoon garlic salt
1 teaspoon dried oregano
1/4 cup freshly grated Parmesan cheese (optional)
2 cups shredded mozzarella cheese

1. *Position the rack to the center of the oven and preheat to 425° F. Lightly grease a 14-1/2- x 10- x 1/2-inch baking sheet. Separate the dinner roll dough and press into the prepared pan, being sure to join the rolls, up to the edge of the pan.*
2. *In a saucepan, combine the chicken, onion, green pepper, mushrooms, and olives. Heat through.*
3. *Spread the pizza sauce over the dough to within 1/2 inch from the edge. Spoon the chicken mixture evenly over the dough to 1/2 inch from the edge, sprinkle with the garlic salt, oregano, and Parmesan cheese. Top with the mozzarella cheese.*
4. *Bake for about 20 minutes or until the crust is puffed and golden brown.*

Mexican Pizza

About 6 to 8 servings

Oil or shortening, for greasing the pan
2 tablespoons cornmeal
1 (10 ounce) can refrigerated prepared pizza dough
1 (7 ounce) bottle taco sauce
1-1/2 cups shredded Monterey Jack cheese
1 cup shredded cheddar cheese
1 pound ground beef, cooked and drained
1/4 cup sliced green onion
1/4 cup sliced black or green olives
1 (4 ounce) can green chiles, drained

1. *Position the oven rack in the center and preheat the oven to 425° F. Lightly grease a round 12-inch pizza pan or a 13- x 9- x 2-inch baking sheet, and sprinkle with the cornmeal.*
2. *Remove the dough from the package, unroll and press it into the prepared baking pan.*
3. *Using a spoon, spread the taco sauce over the crust to 1 inch from the edge. Sprinkle with half of each type of cheese, top with the beef, green onion, olives, and chiles. Evenly sprinkle on the remaining cheese.*
4. *Bake for about 17 to 22 minutes, or until the crust is golden brown. Remove from the oven and set aside for about 5 minutes. Cut into bite-size pieces and serve with sour cream, Guacamole (see page 36), or Black Bean Dip (see page 37), if desired.*

Pepper Pepperoni Pizza

6 to 8 servings

Oil or shortening, for greasing the pan

1 (10 ounce) can refrigerated prepared pizza dough

1 (8 ounce) can tomato sauce, or 8 ounces of your favorite sauce

1 clove garlic, peeled and minced

1-1/2 cups shredded provolone cheese

1/2 (3-1/2 ounce) package sliced pepperoni

1 red bell pepper, stemmed, seeded, and sliced

1 yellow bell pepper, stemmed, seeded, and sliced

1 cup shredded mozzarella or provolone cheese

1. *Position the oven rack in the center and preheat the oven to 425° F. Lightly grease a 12-inch pizza pan.*
2. *Unroll the packaged dough, and press into the prepared pan.*
3. *In a bowl, combine the tomato sauce and garlic. Spoon onto the pizza crust and spread to within 1/2 inch of the edge. Sprinkle with the provolone cheese. Arrange the pepperoni and red and yellow peppers on top, and sprinkle with the mozzarella.*
4. *Bake for about 20 to 23 minutes or until the crust is golden brown. Remove from the oven and let stand for 5 minutes. Cut into wedges or strips and serve.*

1/2 teaspoon of powdered garlic can be used as a substitute for the fresh garlic.

Asian Chicken Spread

8 to 10 servings

3/4 cup diced cooked chicken
1/2 cup shredded carrot
1/4 cup chopped unsalted peanuts
3 tablespoons sliced green onion
1 tablespoon snipped fresh parsley
2 teaspoons lite soy sauce
1/4 teaspoon ginger powder
1 clove garlic, peeled and minced
1/2 cup Great American Sweet and Sour Sauce (see page 127)
1 (8 ounce) package cream cheese, at room temperature
1 tablespoon milk
Assorted crackers, for serving

1. *In a bowl, combine the chicken, carrot, peanuts, green onion, parsley, soy sauce, ginger, and garlic. Cover tightly and refrigerate for at least 2 hours.*
2. *In a second bowl, blend together the cream cheese and milk until smooth. Spread evenly in the bottom of a 10-inch serving dish and spoon the chilled chicken mixture over the top. Drizzle on the Sweet and Sour Sauce, and serve at once with crackers on the side.*

To sweeten the flavor, substitute a honey-soy sauce made with equal parts honey and soy.

Crab Neptune Spread

36 to 40 servings

1/2 cup cottage cheese
1/4 cup sour cream
1/2 cup flaked crab meat (canned crab meat is fine)
1/4 teaspoon curry powder
1/4 cup chopped celery
Salt and pepper, to taste
Crackers or cocktail bread, for serving
2 hard-boiled eggs, shelled, halved widthwise, and thinly sliced lengthwise for garnish

1. *In a bowl, combine the cottage cheese, sour cream, crab meat, curry powder, celery, and salt and pepper to taste. Cover and refrigerate for at least 2 hours.*
2. *When ready, spread evenly on crackers or cocktail bread and garnish with the egg slices. Arrange on a tray and serve.*

Rain Check!
Family Fun for a Rainy Day

Don't let the rain get you down. There are many ways to reclaim a good time when skies are gray. With a supply of family flicks and indoor games, this list of suggestions—for kids and adults—may help get the family back on the happy track.

- GAMES: *all sorts of card games; Monopoly; Scrabble; Twister; Pictionary; 20 Questions; Trivial Pursuit and Junior Trivial Pursuit; and don't forget charades.*

- CLASSIC MOVIES: The Wizard of Oz; It's a Wonderful Life; The Sound of Music; My Fair Lady; Forrest Gump; E.T.; Star Wars; Chitty Chitty Bang Bang; Singin' in the Rain; Pinocchio; Babe; Pete's Dragon; Willy Wonka and the Chocolate Factory; *or animated Disney films such as* Dumbo, Bambi, Aladdin, *and* The Little Mermaid.

★ *You can even combine games and movies to craft a version of charades where players re-enact memorable scenes from their favorite flicks.*

Easy Onion Dip

About 1-1/2 cups

1-1/2 cups cottage cheese

1 tablespoon fresh lemon juice

2 teaspoons granulated sugar

3 tablespoons thinly sliced green onion

Salt and pepper, to taste

In a blender or food processor, combine the cottage cheese, fresh lemon juice, and sugar, and process on low until smooth. Pour into a bowl, and stir in the green onion and salt and pepper to taste. Cover tightly and refrigerate for at least 2 hours and serve alongside crudités or chips.

Curry Dip

About 2 cups

1 cup sour cream

1 cup mayonnaise

1 tablespoon ketchup

2 teaspoons chopped green onion

1/2 to 1 teaspoon curry powder, to taste

1/4 teaspoon garlic salt

1/4 teaspoon Worcestershire sauce

Salt and pepper, to taste

In a bowl, using an electric mixer, beat together the sour cream, mayonnaise, and ketchup until smooth. Stir in the green onion, curry powder to taste, garlic salt, Worcestershire sauce, and salt and pepper to taste. Cover and refrigerate for at least 2 hours or overnight, and serve alongside crudités or chips.

Fresh Garden Dip

About 4 cups

2 cups sour cream

1/2 cup mayonnaise

2 cups chopped cucumber

1/3 cup finely chopped green onion

1/3 cup shredded carrot

1/3 cup chopped radish

Salt and pepper, to taste

In a bowl, using an electric mixer, beat together the sour cream and mayonnaise until smooth. Stir in the cucumber, green onion, carrot, radish, and salt and pepper to taste. Cover and refrigerate for at least 2 hours and serve alongside crudités or chips.

For a stronger onion flavor, substitute green onion with 1 to 2 tablespoons of onion powder.

Verde Vegetable Dip

About 1-1/2 cups

1 cup cottage cheese

1 firmly packed cup parsley sprigs

1/2 cup chopped green onion

1/3 cup capers, drained

2 hard-boiled eggs, shelled and quartered

2 cloves garlic, peeled

1 tablespoon fresh lemon juice

1/4 teaspoon bottled hot sauce

Salt and pepper, to taste

Snipped fresh chives, for garnish

In a blender or food processor, combine the cottage cheese, parsley, green onion, capers, eggs, garlic, fresh lemon juice, hot sauce, and salt and pepper to taste. Process on low until smooth. Pour into a serving bowl, cover, and refrigerate for at least 1 hour. Sprinkle with the chives before serving alongside crudités or assorted chips.

Spicy Peanut Dip

About 2-1/3 cups

2 cups chopped roasted peanuts, see Note
3 large cloves garlic, peeled and halved
1 (2 inch) piece ginger root, peeled and chopped
1/4 cup water
1/4 cup dark sesame oil
1-1/2 teaspoons granulated sugar
3 tablespoons soy sauce
2 tablespoons Chinese rice wine or sake
1-1/2 tablespoons Worcestershire sauce
1 teaspoon hot chili paste
Salt and pepper, to taste

In a blender or food processor, combine the peanuts, garlic, and ginger and process on high for 5 to 8 seconds. Add the water, oil, sugar, soy sauce, rice wine, Worcestershire sauce, chili paste, and salt and pepper and process until just blended. Pour into a bowl and serve alongside fresh snow peas and carrot and celery sticks. This dip is also a delicious accompaniment to skewers of grilled beef, chicken, or tofu.

To "chop" peanuts, place them in a paper bag and smash them with a wooden mallet or rolling pin.

Lemon Pepper Dip

About 2 cups

1 pint sour cream
1-1/2 teaspoons lemon pepper
1 green bell pepper, cored, seeded, and minced
2 tablespoons chopped green onion, whites removed
Salt and pepper, to taste

In a bowl, using an electric mixer, beat together the sour cream, lemon pepper, green pepper, green onion, and salt and pepper to taste until smooth. Pour into a bowl, and serve with fresh fruit or vegetable crudités.

Clam Dip

About 1-1/3 cups

1 (8 ounce) package cream cheese, at room temperature
1 (6-1/2 ounce) can minced clams, drained, with 2 tablespoons
   of the liquid reserved
1 tablespoon minced onion
1 teaspoon snipped fresh parsley
1 tablespoon fresh lemon juice
1 teaspoon Worcestershire sauce
3 drops bottled hot sauce
Salt and pepper, to taste

*In a bowl, using a hand mixer, blend together the cream cheese
and the reserved liquid from the clams. Stir in the clams, onion,
parsley, fresh lemon juice, Worcestershire sauce, hot sauce, and
salt and pepper to taste. Cover and refrigerate for several hours or
overnight. Serve with an assortment of chips and crackers.*

If you'd like to use this as a spread, simply omit the clam liquid.

Keeping Crudités Crisp

Crudités is a French term that broadly refers to raw, crisp vegetables, usually served with a dipping sauce. A well-prepared variety of crudités can add color to your table, but a plate heaped with limp or soggy veggies may leave you pale in the face. Here are a few helpful hints to keep them crisp.

After preparing raw vegetables such as carrots, celery, bell peppers, and broccoli, place the cut sections into zippered plastic bags and store them in the fridge. Avoid cutting smaller items like cherry tomatoes and radishes until serving time. Also, try not to keep the crudités in the coldest part of the fridge—they are susceptible to frost and will turn limp upon thawing. Another no-no: Don't place a pre-arranged platter in the fridge because the vegetables will absorb moisture off the dish. And always serve your crunchy crudités on a bed of crushed ice. Finally, a tip for keeping asparagus and broccoli fresh: Trim the stems and place stalks in a few inches of water. Cover with a plastic bag and refrigerate.

Guacamole

About 4 cups

1/2 cup mayonnaise

1 cup sour cream

3 drops bottled hot sauce

1 tablespoon fresh lime juice

1 teaspoon grated lime zest

2 tablespoons fresh lemon juice

3 ripe avocados, peeled, pitted, and mashed

3 medium tomatoes, peeled, seeded, and diced,
   (see Box on page XXX)

1/2 cup minced white onion or shallots

Fresh parsley sprigs, for garnish

Cayenne pepper to taste, for garnish

1. *In a blender, combine the mayonnaise, sour cream, hot sauce, lime juice, lime zest, and lemon juice and process until smooth. Add the avocado and process on low until just blended.*

2. *Pour into a bowl and stir in the tomatoes and onion. Garnish with parsley and lightly sprinkle with cayenne pepper. Place in the center of a platter and serve with corn or potato chips.*

Roasted Corn & Avocado Dip

About 2-3/4 cups

1 cup frozen whole kernel corn, thawed

2 teaspoons olive oil

2 ripe avocados, peeled and pitted; 1 mashed, 1 chopped

3/4 cup diced seeded tomato

3 tablespoons fresh lime juice

3 tablespoons snipped fresh cilantro leaves

2 tablespoons minced white onion

2 small canned jalapeño peppers, stemmed, seeded, and diced

2 cloves garlic, peeled and minced

1/4 teaspoon ground cumin

Salt and pepper, to taste

1. *Position a rack in the center of the oven and preheat to 400° F.*

2. *In an 8-inch square baking pan, combine the corn and oil, and bake, stirring occasionally, for about 15 minutes or until the corn is lightly browned. Remove from the oven and let cool.*

3. *In a bowl, combine the roasted corn with the remaining ingredients. Serve with a variety of corn tortilla chips.*

Black Bean Dip

About 1-1/2 cups

1 (10-1/2 ounce) can black bean soup
1 (3 ounce) package cream cheese, at room temperature
1/3 cup canned diced tomatoes
2 to 4 tablespoons minced onion
2 to 3 teaspoons chili powder
Salt and pepper, to taste
Chopped tomatoes, green onions, and sour cream, for garnish

1. *In a bowl, using a electric mixer, beat together the soup and cream cheese until smooth. Stir in the tomatoes, onion, chili powder, and salt and pepper to taste.*
2. *Garnish with tomatoes, green onion, and sour cream and serve with tortilla chips.*

Tijuana Taco Dip

10 to 12 servings

Oil or shortening, for greasing the pan
1 (16 ounce) can refried beans
1 (8 ounce) can tomato sauce
1-1/4 teaspoons bottled hot sauce
1 large tomato, cored and chopped
3/4 cup shredded Monterey Jack cheese
3/4 cup ground beef
2 teaspoons chili powder
Salt and pepper, to taste
1 cup sliced black olives
1 cup shredded cheddar cheese
1 cup sour cream
Chopped green onion, olives, and tomatoes, for garnish

1. *Position a rack in the center and preheat oven to 350° F. Lightly grease a 1-1/2-quart casserole baking dish.*
2. *In a bowl, combine the refried beans, 3 tablespoons of the tomato sauce, and 1/2 teaspoon of the hot sauce, and stir until smooth. Spread evenly into a 1-1/2-quart baking dish and top with the chopped tomatoes and Monterey Jack cheese.*
3. *In a skillet over medium heat, sauté the beef until no longer pink. Stir in the chili powder, remove from the heat, and drain off any excess fat. Stir in the remaining tomato sauce, black olives, remaining hot sauce, and salt and pepper to taste.*
4. *Spread the beef mixture evenly over the casserole. Sprinkle with the cheddar cheese and bake for about 15 to 20 minutes or until both cheeses have melted and the beans are hot.*
5. *Remove from the oven and let cool slightly. Spread the sour cream over the top, garnish with the green onion, olives, and tomatoes, and serve warm with tortilla chips.*

The Salad Bowl

Picnic in the Park

SIPS AND STARTERS

•

Cranberry Quencher
Black Bean Dip
Rolled Tortilla Bites

SALADS

•

Asparagus & Spinach Salad
Tomato Cucumber Salad
Jane's Melon Salad

ENTREES

•

Crispy Honey Dip't Chicken
Grilled Tofu Sandwiches with Red Onion-Cucumber Salsa

SIDES

•

Confetti Barley

FROM THE BAKERY

•

Cherry Chocolate Cupcakes

The Simplest Green Salad

6 to 8 servings

2 medium heads iceberg lettuce, rinsed, dried, stems
   and ribs removed
1 to 2 tablespoons fresh lemon or lime juice
6 to 7 tablespoons extra virgin olive oil
Salt and pepper, to taste

1. *In a bowl, combine the lemon juice, olive oil, and salt and
   pepper to taste. Using a wire whisk, beat vigorously until
   slightly cloudy.*
2. *Place the lettuce in a large bowl and drizzle the dressing
   over it, tossing gently to coat.*

If you do not plan to serve a green salad immediately, the dry, undressed lettuce can be placed in zippered plastic bags and refrigerated until ready.

Lettuce Salad Bowl

About 12 servings

1/2 (10 ounce) package frozen green peas
1 small head romaine lettuce, rinsed, dried, and torn into
   bite-size pieces
1 small head iceberg lettuce, rinsed, dried, and torn into
   bite-size pieces
1 small cucumber, trimmed and thinly sliced
3 green onions, washed, trimmed, and chopped with tops
2 stalks celery with greens, chopped
Poppyseed Dressing, for serving (see page 142)

1. *Place the peas in a bowl, cover with boiling water and set aside
   for 5 minutes to thaw. Drain.*
2. *In a bowl, combine the peas, lettuce, cucumber, green onion,
   and celery and toss gently. Drizzle on the Poppyseed Dressing
   or the dressing of your choice.*

Asparagus & Spinach Salad

6 to 8 servings

1/2 pound fresh spinach leaves

12 to 14 young asparagus spears, tough ends removed, chopped
    into 2-inch pieces

2 tablespoons butter or margarine

Bottled vinaigrette, for serving

1. *Thoroughly wash the spinach under running water, and use a sharp knife to trim away and discard the stems and tough center core. Pat dry using paper towel, and place in a plastic bag in the refrigerator until needed.*
2. *Melt the butter in a skillet, and sauté the asparagus until tender but still crisp. Transfer to a paper towel to drain.*
3. *In a bowl, combine the spinach and asparagus, drizzle with the vinaigrette, and toss gently to coat.*

European Green Salad

6 to 8 servings

1 medium head arugula

3 small heads endive

2 heads radicchio

1/2 pound fresh spinach

1/2 cup crumbled feta cheese

Mustard-Chive Vinaigrette, for serving (see page 142)

1. *Thoroughly rinse and pat dry the arugula, endive, radicchio, and spinach leaves. Using a sharp knife, trim away and discard the white tough portions of the leaves and roughly chop the endive.*
2. *Combine the greens in a large plastic bag and toss gently. Place in the refrigerator to chill until needed.*
3. *When ready to serve, add the crumbled feta, drizzle on the Mustard-Chive Vinaigrette and toss gently to coat.*

Get Clean, Gritty Green

Spinach grows on short stems close to the ground in sandy soil that clings to its leaves. Like all greens, wash spinach as soon as you bring it home from market. Cut the stems off and place the spinach in a sink filled with cold water. Swish around thoroughly and let the grit settle to the bottom of the sink before removing to dry.

Sante Fe Salad

6 to 8 servings

3 large ripe avocados, peeled and pitted; 1 diced, 2 sliced

1/2 cup sour cream

4 tablespoons fresh lemon juice

1 tablespoon minced shallots

1 tablespoon white wine or water

1/4 teaspoon bottled hot sauce

6 cups torn, cleaned lettuce leaves

2 large tomatoes, stemmed and diced

1 cup shredded cheddar cheese

1/2 cup sliced pitted olives, for garnish

1 cup crushed tortilla chips, for garnish

1. *In a blender, combine the diced avocado, sour cream, 3 table-spoons of the lemon juice, shallots, wine, and hot sauce and process on medium until smooth. Transfer to a bowl, cover tightly, and chill for at least 3 hours.*
2. *In a large bowl, sprinkle the remaining lemon juice over the sliced avocado and toss very gently to coat. On top, layer the lettuce, tomatoes, cheese, and olives. Cover tightly and chill in the refrigerator.*
3. *When ready, drizzle the dressing over the salad and toss gently to coat. Garnish with the olives and tortilla chips and serve.*

Spinach Salad with Sherry-Cumin Vinaigrette

6 to 8 servings

1/4 cup sherry vinegar

1 tablespoon Dijon mustard

1 tablespoon plus 1 teaspoon honey

1 tablespoon ground cumin, or to taste

3/4 cup extra virgin olive oil

Salt and pepper, to taste

2 (6 ounce) bags baby spinach leaves

3 plum tomatoes, stemmed and sliced

3 hard-boiled eggs, shelled and sliced

2 ripe avocados, peeled, pitted, and sliced

1 red onion, peeled and thinly sliced

1. *In a small bowl, whisk together the vinegar, mustard, honey, cumin, olive oil, and salt and pepper to taste.*
2. *In a large bowl, combine the spinach, tomatoes, egg, avocado, and onion. Drizzle with the vinaigrette and toss gently to coat.*

The Playing Field: Perfect Picnic Games & Activities

Picnics are packed with great eats, but you don't just have to fill your basket with food. There are a number of games and activities that can be fun for all ages at your next buffet-on-a-blanket.

- WIFFLE BALL: *A plastic version of baseball, wiffle ball offers a great warm-up for youngsters interested in the popular pastime. Just set up a makeshift field with rags for bases, and play ball!*

- CHESS, CHECKERS, BACKGAMMON, *or* CARDS: *Lay your blanket out on a flat patch of grass, and relax to a game of chess, checkers, backgammon, or cards. Bring pillows for back support. Or take a couple of outdoor chairs and a small table.*

- KITE-FLYING: *Let your spirit fly when you unreel a kite to the winds. The old hobby has become increasingly sophisticated and an unbelievable variety of kites are on the market these days. Some are designed with multiple handles and numerous intricacies to hone your skills in navigating the kite; others to simply watch the kite do its thing while your daydreaming plays out against a backdrop of blue sky.*

- HUMAN KNOT: *Gather 'round as many players as possible in a tight circle. Each player grabs hands with two others at random. Hold on tight. It's the group's mission to untangle this human knot, and although there are no winners or losers, a whole lot of twisting and squirming will go on.*

- SHOE SWAP: *Now this may seem a little too much like the ridiculous ploy of those hokey fraternity boys in the 1950s, but the shoe swap is a surefire laugh-out-loud mix-up. Separate players into two teams; remove shoes and jumble them together in a pile. When the start is called, both teams race to put their shoes on. The first team with all players wearing their shoes wins.*

Green Salad with Watermelon

6 to 8 servings

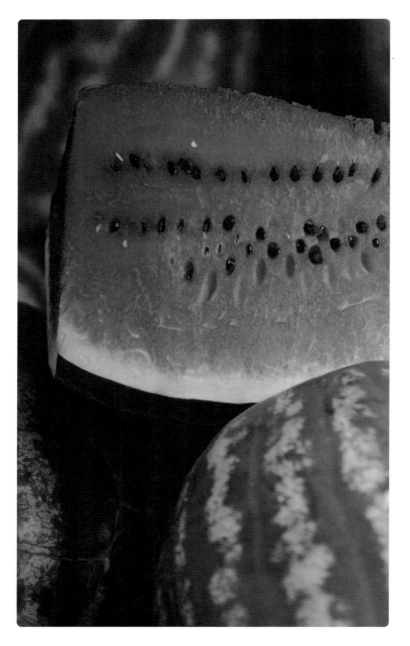

1 large head romaine lettuce
1/4 cup red wine vinegar
3/4 cup extra virgin olive oil
2 tablespoons raspberry jam
Salt and pepper, to taste
1 small red onion, peeled and thinly sliced
1 pint fresh raspberries, rinsed and patted dry
3 cups cubed seedless watermelon
1/2 cup crumbled feta cheese

1. *Approximately 2 hours before serving, separate and thoroughly wash the lettuce leaves and cut into bite-size pieces. Place in a zippered plastic bag, and chill in the coldest area of the refrigerator until needed.*
2. *In a blender, combine the vinegar, olive oil, and raspberry jam and process on low until smooth. Add salt and pepper to taste and set aside.*
3. *In a bowl, combine the onion, raspberries, and watermelon. Cover and chill in the refrigerator until ready.*
4. *To assemble, combine the lettuce and fruit, drizzle with the dressing, and toss to coat. Serve in chilled salad bowls garnished with the feta cheese.*

Greens with Mixed Berries

6 to 8 servings

1 head bibb lettuce, separated, rinsed, and patted dry

1/2 pint fresh strawberries, rinsed, stemmed, and sliced

1/2 pint fresh blueberries, rinsed and stemmed

About 18 fresh raspberries, rinsed and stemmed

About 18 fresh blackberries, rinsed and stemmed

1 large cucumber, peeled, halved lengthwise, seeded, and cut into
   1/4-inch slices

1 bundle watercress, broken into small sprigs and rinsed

1 tablespoon minced shallots

1. *Arrange bibb lettuce leaves around a large serving bowl.*
2. *In another bowl, combine the strawberries, blueberries, raspberries, and blackberries. Cover tightly and refrigerate for at least 2 hours.*
3. *When ready, spoon the fruit into the center of the lettuce leaves, arrange the cucumber slices around the edge, top each slice with a sprig of watercress. Garnish with the shallots and serve with a dressing of your choice on the side.*

So Berry Delicious: Picking & Storing the Summer's Bounty

Berries are living proof of the old adage: Good things come in small packages. Berries grow in a variety of climates but are generally known as a northern fruit. Many, especially strawberries, are commercially cultivated, but all seem to convey a sense of the wooded wilderness. In fact, many wild berries taste better than anything at your favorite fruit stand. But at market, closely examine the area where the stem meets the berry. Obviously, avoid bruised-looking fruit. Most should be firm but not resistant to pressure. Wash your berries once you get home, pat them dry with paper towels, and place them in moisture-proof wrapping or zippered plastic bags to store them in the fridge. Most varieties should be eaten within two days.

Watercress & Carrot Salad

6 to 8 servings

2 bunches fresh watercress

6 medium carrots, trimmed, peeled, and julienned

3/4 cup virgin olive oil

1/4 cup fresh lime juice

1 tablespoon granulated sugar

1/4 teaspoon paprika

1/4 teaspoon dry mustard

Salt and pepper, to taste

1. *Thoroughly rinse and pat dry the watercress. Cut away the tough ends from the stems and tear the sprigs into bite-size pieces.*
2. *In a bowl, combine the watercress and carrots.*
3. *In a small bowl, whisk together the oil, juice, sugar, paprika, mustard, and salt and pepper to taste. Drizzle over the salad, toss gently to coat, and serve immediately.*

If possible, freshly-picked watercress should be used because it is more flavorful.

Holiday Salad

6 to 8 servings

1 tablespoon toasted sesame seeds

2 tablespoons red wine vinegar

2 teaspoons granulated sugar

2 teaspoons minced fresh ginger

1/4 teaspoon minced garlic

1/4 cup soy sauce

1 cup julienne radishes

1 cup julienne cucumbers

4 cups shredded iceberg lettuce

Salt and pepper, to taste

1. *In a bowl, whisk together the sesame seeds, vinegar, sugar, ginger, garlic, and soy sauce until smooth.*
2. *In another bowl, combine the radish, cucumber, and lettuce. Cover tightly, and refrigerate for at least 1 hour.*
3. *Remove the salad from the refrigerator and drizzle on the dressing, tossing gently to coat. Add salt and pepper to taste and serve.*

Tropical Salad

6 to 8 servings

1 tablespoon lime zest

3 tablespoons fresh lime juice

2 tablespoons extra virgin olive oil

2 tablespoons warm honey

Salt and pepper, to taste

1 medium papaya, peeled, halved, and seeded

1 (13 ounce) can hearts of palm, drained

1 bunch watercress, rinsed and dried

2 tablespoons toasted pine nuts, see Note

1. *In a bowl, whisk together the zest, juice, oil, and warm honey until smooth. Adjust the salt and pepper to taste, and refrigerate for at least 2 hours.*
2. *Using a sharp knife, cut the papaya lengthwise into about 15 thin slices and arrange on individual serving plates.*
3. *Cut the hearts of palm into thin diagonal slices and arrange on top of the papaya slices.*
4. *Break the watercress into small sprigs and arrange around the edges of the serving plates.*
5. *Drizzle some of the dressing over each plate, sprinkle with pine nuts, and serve.*

Taste pine nuts in a dry pan over medium heat.

Broccoli-Cauliflower Salad with Green Goddess Dressing

8 to 10 servings

2/3 cup bottled Green Goddess dressing

1/3 cup mayonnaise

2 tablespoons red wine vinegar

1 teaspoon anise seeds

2 cups broccoli florets

3-1/2 cups cauliflower florets

1 medium red onion, peeled and thinly sliced

1/2 cup chopped plum tomatoes

1. *In a bowl, whisk together the Green Goddess dressing, mayonnaise, vinegar, and anise seeds until smooth.*
2. *Add the broccoli, cauliflower and onions, and toss gently to coat. Cover tightly and chill in the refrigerator.*
3. *Bring to room temperature and top with tomatoes before serving.*

Fresh Tomato Salad

6 to 8 servings

1 pound ripe Beefsteak or vine tomatoes

18 romaine lettuce leaves

1/4 cup chopped chives or green onion

Salt and pepper, to taste

Zucchini or pumpkin blossoms, for garnish (optional)

1. *Blanch the tomatoes: Drop them one at a time into a pot of boiling water, remove them immediately, and immerse in a pan of ice-cold water. Pull off the skin and use a sharp knife to slice into 1/4-inch slices. Place in a bowl, cover, and chill.*
2. *Separate the lettuce leaves, and wash thoroughly. Using a sharp knife, cut away and discard the tough white ends. Slice the leaves crosswise into 1/2-inch pieces.*
3. *Arrange the tomatoes on a large platter, surround with the lettuce, and sprinkle with chopped chives. Add salt and pepper to taste and garnish with zucchini blossoms if desired.*

Tomato Cucumber Salad

6 to 8 servings

3/4 cup extra virgin olive oil

1/4 cup red wine vinegar

1 tablespoon snipped fresh parsley

1 teaspoon crushed dried dill

2 tablespoons grated fresh shallots

Dash bottled hot sauce

3 medium tomatoes, stemmed and thinly sliced

2 medium cucumbers, thinly sliced

1 small head romaine lettuce, rinsed, dried, and torn into
   bite-size pieces

1. *In a blender or food processor, combine the oil, vinegar, parsley, dill, shallots, and hot sauce and process on low for a few seconds to blend.*
2. *Place the tomatoes in a bowl and drizzle with the dressing. Cover and refrigerate for at least 1 hour.*
3. *Add the cucumber and lettuce to the tomatoes just before serving and toss gently.*

Tomato & Mozzarella Salad with Green & Purple Basil

4 to 6 servings

2 pounds plum or vine-ripened tomatoes
1 pound fresh mozzarella
1/2 cup green basil leaves, rinsed and patted dry
1/2 cup purple basil leaves, rinsed and patted dry
Salt and pepper, to taste
Extra virgin olive oil and balsamic vinegar, to taste

1. *Rinse and pat dry the tomatoes and slice 1/4 inch thick.*
2. *Slice the mozzarella 1/4 inch thick.*
3. *Arrange the tomatoes and mozzarella on a large plate and sprinkle the basil leaves on top. Season with salt and pepper and oil and vinegar, to taste.*

Old-Fashioned Backyard Egg Toss

What better way to get rid of those pesky eggs sitting at the bottom of the fridge than an old-fashioned egg toss? Granted, the eggs may not be pesky, but still, fun is fun, and the egg toss has always been a favorite for kids and adults alike. Set up two parallel lines of egg-players, a partner at each end. Start from a few feet away. After two consecutive tosses, both players should take a step back before the next challenge. A referee can help keep your lines straight. And if you're one of the players, here's a little secret: Try to secure a hard-boiled egg for your team so you don't end up looking like an omelet! At the end, hand out prizes to everyone, or to the people who are the least eggy.

Macaroni Salad

4 to 6 servings

1 cup elbow macaroni, cooked al dente, and drained

2 (8 ounce) cans sliced mushrooms, drained

2 tablespoons fresh lemon juice

2 tablespoons extra virgin olive oil

1 medium clove garlic, peeled and minced

2/3 cup sour cream or plain yogurt

2/3 cup mayonnaise

1 tablespoon snipped fresh chervil

1. *In a bowl, combine the pasta and mushrooms.*
2. *In a blender, combine the lemon juice, olive oil, garlic, sour cream, mayonnaise, and chervil, and process on low until smooth.*
3. *Drizzle the dressing over the pasta, and toss gently to coat. Cover and refrigerate for at least 1 hour before serving.*

Pasta Salad Primavera

About 6 servings

4 tablespoons olive oil, divided

1 medium onion, peeled and chopped

1 zucchini, trimmed, and chopped

1 cup broccoli florets

1 cup frozen green peas, thawed

1 clove garlic, peeled and minced

1 pound rotini pasta, cooked al dente, and drained

3 plum tomatoes, stemmed, seeded, and chopped

Salt and pepper, to taste

1. *In a large saucepan, heat 2 tablespoons of the olive oil over medium heat.*
2. *Add the onion, zucchini, and broccoli and sauté until tender, about 7 minutes.*
3. *Add the peas and garlic and sauté until the garlic is golden.*
4. *In a large bowl, toss together the sautéed vegetables, pasta, and tomatoes with the remaining 2 tablespoons of oil. Season with salt and pepper to taste, and serve at room temperature.*

Herbed Roasted Potato Salad

6 to 8 servings

Classic Potato Salad

6 to 8 servings

Oil or butter, for greasing the pan

2 pounds small red potatoes, scrubbed and quartered

1/4 cup olive oil

Salt and pepper, to taste

1 tablespoon snipped fresh chives

1 teaspoon snipped fresh thyme

1 large head garlic, outer skin intact, tip removed

1 tablespoon balsamic vinegar

1/2 cup chopped, pitted black olives

1/4 cup chopped, pitted green olives

1. *Position a rack in the center of the oven and preheat to 425° F. Lightly grease a 13- x 9- x 2-inch baking pan.*
2. *In the prepared baking pan, combine the potatoes, olive oil, salt and pepper to taste, rosemary, thyme, and garlic. Cover tightly with foil and bake for about 20 minutes. Remove the foil and continue to bake for about 20 minutes longer, or until the potatoes start to brown. Remove from the oven and let cool for about 15 minutes.*
3. *Transfer the head of garlic to a cutting board and squeeze the cloves out of the skin. Mash the cloves using a fork or the back of a spoon.*
4. *In a serving bowl, combine the mashed garlic, vinegar, and olives. Add the potatoes and any juices from the pan, and toss gently to coat. Serve immediately.*

6 medium to large boiled potatoes, chilled, peeled, and cubed

4 large hard-boiled eggs, chilled, shelled, and diced

1/4 cup diced green bell pepper

1 cup minced onion

2 stalks celery, diced

1 cup mayonnaise

Salt and pepper, to taste

In a large bowl, combine all of the ingredients, and toss gently until coated with mayonnaise. Cover tightly and chill in the refrigerator for at least 1 hour before serving.

VARIATION 1:
Use a combination of red and green peppers, and add 1/4 cup cooked whole kernel corn.

VARIATION 2:
Add sliced mushrooms, crushed walnuts or pecans, and substitute a creamy salad dressing for the mayonnaise.

VARIATION 3:
Combine 1/2 cup mayonnaise with 1/2 cup light cream, 1-1/2 tablespoons white wine vinegar, and a pinch of fresh dill and fresh marjoram.

VARIATION 4:
Stir in fresh crumbled bacon and serve on a bed of lettuce, garnished with fresh lemon slices.

Summer Rice Salad

6 to 8 servings

1 (8 ounce) package cream cheese

4 to 5 tablespoons soy milk

1 tablespoon granulated sugar

1/2 teaspoon anise seeds

3 cups cooked jasmine or basmati rice

5 medium tomatoes, peeled, seeded, and diced (see Box, page 66)

2 small zucchini, trimmed and diced

3 green onions, sliced

3 tablespoons crushed pecans

Salt and pepper, to taste

1. *In a blender or food processor, combine the cream cheese, soy milk, sugar, and anise seeds and process on low until smooth and creamy. (Additional soy milk can be used to achieve the desired consistency.)*
2. *In a large bowl, combine the rice, tomatoes, zucchini, green onions, and pecans. Drizzle on the sauce and toss gently to coat. Add salt and pepper to taste, and serve.*

Aunt Betty's Pasta Shrimp Salad

4 to 6 servings

1/2 cup mayonnaise

2 large eggs, hard-boiled, shelled, and chopped

Salt and pepper, to taste

3 (6 ounce) cans tiny deveined shrimp, drained

4 cups cooked miniature pasta shells

2 medium tomatoes, stemmed and diced

1. *In a bowl, whisk together the mayonnaise, egg, and salt and pepper to taste. Cover tightly and refrigerate for at least 1 hour.*
2. *Thoroughly rinse the shrimp under running water, and pat dry using paper towels.*
3. *In another bowl, combine the shrimp, pasta shells, and tomatoes. Cover tightly and refrigerate until needed.*
4. *Fluff up the mayonnaise mixture with a whisk and spoon over the shrimp and pasta. Toss gently to coat and serve.*

Red and Green Slaw

6 to 8 servings

2 cups finely chopped broccoli florets

2 cups shredded red cabbage

2 cups shredded green cabbage

3/4 cup unsweetened apple juice

1/3 cup extra virgin olive oil

3 tablespoons red wine vinegar

2 small cloves garlic, peeled

Salt and pepper, to taste

1. *In a large bowl, toss together the broccoli and cabbages.*
2. *In a blender, combine the apple juice, olive oil, vinegar, and garlic and process on high until smooth. Add salt and pepper to taste.*
3. *Drizzle the dressing over the slaw and toss to coat. Cover tightly and refrigerate for at least 1 hour before serving.*

Deluxe Coleslaw

6 to 8 servings

1 medium head cabbage, shredded or thinly sliced

1 large tart apple, cored, chopped,
   and sprinkled with fresh lemon juice

2 large carrots, peeled and shredded

1 stalk celery, thinly sliced

2 tablespoons mayonnaise

1 cup sour cream

1 tablespoon sugar

1 tablespoon amaretto liqueur

1/2 teaspoon honey soy sauce (see page 28)

1. *In a plastic bag, combine the cabbage, apple, carrots, and celery and toss gently.*
2. *In a blender or food processor, combine the mayonnaise, sour cream, sugar, amaretto, and honey soy sauce, and process on low until smooth.*
3. *Pour the mayonnaise mixture over the cabbage mixture, toss to coat, and serve.*

Alsatian Cabbage Slaw

6 to 8 servings

1/2 pound bacon
2 cups red onion, chopped
1/2 cup cider vinegar
1 medium head cabbage, cored and shredded

In a skillet, sauté the bacon until crisp. Transfer to a rack covered with paper towels, let cool slightly, and then crumble. In the drippings, sauté the onion until tender. Add the vinegar, turn heat to low, and add the cabbage and bacon, tossing lightly to incorporate. Remove from the heat and serve.

Cilantro Slaw with Garlic Dressing

About 6 servings

1 small head of white cabbage, finely shredded
2 tablespoons snipped fresh cilantro
1 medium cucumber, peeled, seeded, and coarsely shredded
1 small yellow onion, minced
1/2 cup bottled roasted garlic or Caesar salad dressing

In a bowl, toss together the cabbage, cilantro, cucumber, onion, and salad dressing. Cover with plastic wrap and refrigerate for about 1 hour before serving.

The Scoop on Slaw

Coleslaw made its debut in English dictionaries in the late 1700s. The Dutch are often credited with introducing the cabbage concoction since it took its name from *koosla*, a shortened form for *kool-salade*. In Dutch, the word *kool* means cabbage, and the original dish was probably served hot. It was Richard Hellman who popularized the current cold version in New York, when he began marketing his own bottled mayonnaise in 1912. Needless to say, his creamy condiment enjoyed success and became a favorite dressing for shredded cabbage.

Strawberry Citrus Salad

6 to 8 servings

1 cup mandarin orange segments

1 cup diced fresh pineapple

1 cup fresh strawberries, rinsed, stemmed, and halved

1 cup grapefruit segments

1/2 cup maple syrup, warm

1/4 cup honey, warm

Small head of lettuce, separated, rinsed, and patted dry

2 large bananas, peeled and sliced

1. *In a large bowl, combine the orange, pineapple, strawberries, and grapefruit.*
2. *Combine the warm maple syrup and honey, drizzle over the fruit, and toss gently to coat. Cover tightly and refrigerate for 1 hour, or up to 1 day.*
3. *When ready to serve, arrange the lettuce leaves on a platter and top with the fruit salad and banana slices.*

Hawaiian Fruit Salad

6 to 8 servings

1/4 cup fresh lime juice

1/4 cup corn syrup

4 medium papayas

4 medium bananas, peeled

1/4 cup shredded sweetened coconut

1/4 cup minced preserved ginger in syrup,
    drained, with syrup reserved

1. *In a bowl, blend together the lime juice, corn syrup, and 1/4 cup of the preserved ginger syrup.*
2. *Using a sharp knife, cut the papayas in half lengthwise and scoop out the seeds. Cut a thin slice from the papayas' peel sides, so the papayas will sit flat on their backs like bowls. Arrange on a serving platter.*
3. *Quarter the bananas lengthwise, divide between the papaya bowls, and sprinkle with the coconut and preserved ginger. Drizzle with the dressing and serve.*

Jane's Melon Salad

8 to 10 servings

1 honeydew melon, pitted, peeled and coarsely chopped
1/2 watermelon, balled
3 large cantaloupes, pitted, peeled and sliced
Zest of 1 lime
Candied ginger, chopped, for garnish
Fresh Lime Dressing, for serving (see page 142)

In a large bowl, combine the melon, lime zest, and ginger.
Cover tightly and chill in the refrigerator for at least 4 hours.
Serve with Lime Dressing on the side.

Mind Your Melons

Succulent and sweet, melons are a joy to the taste buds, but it can be difficult to select a ripe fruit from among the array of melons at the market. When ripe, most muskmelons, such as cantaloupe and honeydew, are slightly soft on the bottom and emit a subtle, fruity perfume. For muskmelons and watermelons alike, avoid fruit with flat sides. Better to pick symmetrical melons. For watermelons, the rind should be dull instead of shiny in appearance; slap its side to listen for the sound of a hollow thump—ripe music to the ears.

Royal Fruit Salad

6 to 8 servings

1 cup pitted frozen cherries, thawed and halved

1 (12 ounce) package frozen green grapes, thawed and halved

1 (14 ounce) can bartlett pears, drained and diced

1 (14 ounce) can peaches, drained and diced

1/2 cup crushed pineapple

2 tablespoons confectioner's sugar

1/2 cup pineapple juice

1/2 cup mayonnaise

1 cup berry-flavored yogurt or plain sour cream, whipped

1. *In a bowl, combine the cherries, grapes, pears, peaches, and pineapple. Cover and refrigerate for at least 2 hours.*
2. *In a blender, combine the sugar, pineapple juice, mayonnaise, and yogurt. Process on low until smooth.*
3. *When ready to serve, combine the fruit and dressing and toss.*

Fresh green grapes can be substituted for the frozen, if desired.

Sacramento Fruit Bowls

6 to 8 servings

1 (8 ounce) package cream cheese

1/4 cup milk or soy milk

3 tablespoons sugar

3 tablespoons lime or fresh lemon juice

3/4 teaspoon ground cardamom

2-1/2 cups diced honeydew melon

1-1/2 cups diced cantaloupe

6 medium plums, blanched, peeled, pitted, and sliced
(see Box, page 66)

2 medium pears, blanched, peeled, cored, and diced
(see Box, page 66)

3 medium peaches, blanched, peeled, pitted, and sliced
(see Box, page 66)

1. *In a blender, combine the cream cheese, milk, sugar, lime juice, and cardamom and process on low until smooth.*
2. *In a large bowl, combine the fruit and drizzle on a small portion of the dressing, tossing gently to coat. Cover tightly and refrigerate for at least 2 hours.*
3. *Serve in chilled bowls with the remaining dressing on the side.*

Ambrosia Fruit Salad

About 20 servings

2 (11 ounce) cans mandarin oranges, drained

2 (40 ounce) cans pineapple tidbits, drained

2 large bananas, peeled and sliced

2 cups seedless grapes

1 cup slivered almonds

2 cups flaked coconut

2 cups mini marshmallows

1–2 cups vanilla or chocolate yogurt

1. *In a large bowl, combine the oranges, pineapple, banana, grapes, almonds, coconut, marshmallows, and 1 cup of the yogurt. The chunky ingredients should be well-coated—add additional yogurt if desired. Cover tightly and refrigerate for at least 4 hours.*
2. *When ready, spoon into chilled glasses and garnish with a sprinkle of additional coconut on top.*

Slightly softened ice cream or whipped cream can be used in place of the yogurt.

Blanching: A Relaxing Spa for Tense Ingredients

A quick soak in a hot tub may be just the right thing to relieve muscle tension. Likewise, blanching can be a great way to relax an ingredient prior to some subsequent preparation. A common method of partially cooking an ingredient in boiling water, blanching can prevent off-flavors, discoloration, and nutrient loss. Still, you need to know what you're doing to give your food just the right "soak in the tub."

"Pre-soak" preparations: Core tomatoes with a paring knife. For other fruits, such as peaches, just remove the stem. Carefully slit an X in the bottom of round fruits, just penetrating the skin, before placing in boiling water for 20–30 seconds. Remove and plunge into a cold water bath. When the fruit has cooled enough to handle, use the edge of a knife to slip off the skin.

Mixed Melon JELL-O Nut Salad

6 to 8 servings

1 (3 ounce) package watermelon-flavored gelatin

1 cup boiling water

1/2 cup cold water

1 teaspoon fresh lemon juice

1 (3 ounce) package cream cheese, at room temperature

2 tablespoons mayonnaise

1 cup diced cantaloupe or small cantaloupe balls,
   halved melon rinds reserved

1/4 cup finely slivered almonds

1. *In a bowl or blender, combine the gelatin and boiling water and mix until the gelatin is dissolved. Add the cold water and lemon juice, and divide into two equal portions. Place one portion in the coldest area of the refrigerator and chill until very thick, but not firm. Cover the second portion and leave at room temperature.*

2. *Meanwhile, in another bowl, stir together the cream cheese and mayonnaise until smooth, then fold into the room temperature portion of gelatin.*

3. *When the refrigerated gelatin is ready, add the cantaloupe and almonds and spoon into the empty melon rinds or a 2–3-quart mold of choice. Return to the refrigerator until set. Spoon in the cream cheese portion and chill until the entire mold is set.*

To keep the room temperature portion of the gelatin from setting up too firmly, place it in a bowl of warm water.

Hello JELL-O

Having celebrated its centennial anniversary in 1997, JELL-O's been around since long before Bill Cosby. And it's likely to remain for some time to come. According to Kraft Foods, more than a million packages of JELL-O gelatin are purchased or eaten each day, and JELL-O gelatin is the world's most popular dessert, with more than 500 million boxes purchased annually.

Originally, JELL-O was only available in strawberry, raspberry, orange, and lemon flavors. Today, it comes in more than 20 different flavors, and is available in sugar-free as well. You can cash in on this upwardly mobile product during special occasions thanks to the fact that JELL-O can be molded. Create crazy shapes with your dessert to fit a theme for a party, for holidays, or just for fun. On Kraft's website, they promote custom-made molds of Halloween ghouls and Christmastime gingerbread men, and in all the letters of the alphabet. You can also easily find your own mold at any restaurant supply or kitchenware store.

For classic JELL-O recipes, check out the website at www.jello.com. And why not add fruits and nuts to liven up an old favorite? This is a fun food—play around with it.

From the Grill

Backyard Barbecue

SIPS AND STARTERS

•

Fruity Fruit Cup Punch
Roasted Corn & Avocado Dip

SALADS

•

Green Salad with Watermelon
European Green Salad

ENTREES

•

The Perfect Burger
Grilled Sausage

SIDES

Classic Potato Salad
Savory Grilled Tomatoes
Grilled Corn on the Cob

FROM THE BAKERY

•

Double Chocolate Brownies

The Perfect Burger

8 servings

2 pounds lean ground beef
2 tablespoons soy flour (white flour is okay, if soy flour is unavailable)
1 teaspoon garlic powder
1 teaspoon onion powder
Salt and pepper, to taste
Vegetable oil, for brushing
Barbecue Sauce (see pages 122 to 124), for basting
Hamburger buns
Lettuce, sliced ripe tomato, sliced red onion, for garnish (optional)

1. *In a bowl, gently knead together the beef, soy flour, garlic powder, onion powder, and salt and pepper to taste. (Be careful not to handle the meat too much, or it will become tough.) Cover with plastic wrap and refrigerate until ready to cook.*
2. *Arrange the briquettes in the barbecue, position the grill rack 6 inches from the heat source, brush lightly with vegetable oil, and preheat to high.*
3. *Divide the meat mixture into 8 equal parts, and form each into a burger about 1/4-inch thick. Brush each burger with a little oil.*
4. *Arrange the burgers on the grill rack and cook, basting with barbecue sauce and turning, for about 10 to 12 minutes, or until cooked as desired. Remove from the barbecue, place on buns and garnish with lettuce, tomato, and onion. Serve immediately.*

Burgers Five Ways

About 4 servings

Vegetable oil, for the rack
1 pound lean ground beef
Salt and pepper, to taste
1 tablespoon dried minced onion
Pinch garlic powder
4 hamburger buns, for serving

1. Arrange the briquettes in the barbecue, position the grill rack 4 to 6 inches from the heat source, brush lightly with vegetable oil, and preheat to high.
2. In a bowl, gently knead together the beef, salt and pepper, onions, and garlic powder. (Be careful not to handle the meat too much or it will become tough.) Divide into four equal patties.
3. Arrange the burgers on the grill rack and cook for about 3 to 4 minutes per side, or until cooked as desired. Remove from the grill, place on buns, and serve.

VARIATIONS:

1. Chili Cheeseburgers: Add 1 cup grated cheese, 1/4 cup milk, and 1/2 teaspoon chili powder.
2. Dill Olive Burgers: Add 1/2 teaspoon crushed dried dill and 1/4 cup chopped olives.
3. Thai Burgers: Add 1/2 teaspoon ginger powder, 1 teaspoon lemon zest, 1 teaspoon soy sauce.
4. Savory Burgers: Add 1/2 teaspoon crushed dried basil, 1/2 teaspoon crushed dried tarragon, and 1/4 teaspoon crushed dried savory.

Teriyaki Burgers

6 servings

1-1/2 pounds lean ground beef
1 (8 ounce) can sliced water chestnuts, drained and finely chopped
1/4 cup Teriyaki Marinade (see page 139), or bottled teriyaki sauce
Vegetable oil, for the rack
6 sandwich buns, toasted

1. In a bowl, gently knead together the ground beef and water chestnuts. (Be careful not to handle the meat too much or it will become tough.) Divide into 6 equal parts, shape each into a ball, and flatten to a thickness of 1/2 inch. Place in a 13- x 9-inch baking pan.
2. Pour the Teriyaki Marinade over the burgers, cover with plastic wrap, and refrigerate for at 3 to 5 hours.
3. Arrange briquettes in the barbecue, lightly oil the grill rack, and preheat to high.
4. When ready, transfer the burgers to the grill and cook 4 to 6 inches from the coals, turning only once, and brushing with the marinade for about 10 to 15 minutes, or until cooked as desired. Remove from the heat, and serve on toasted buns.

Hawaiian Burgers

4 to 6 servings

1-1/2 pounds ground turkey or chicken
1/2 cup fine dry bread crumbs
1 tablespoon honey soy sauce (see Note)
1/2 teaspoon ginger powder
1 cup prepared sweet and sour sauce
Vegetable oil, for the rack
6 pineapple slices (canned is okay)
1 (8 ounce) can crushed pineapple, drained
4 to 6 hamburger buns, split

1. *In a bowl, gently knead together the turkey, bread crumbs, soy sauce, ginger powder, and 1/4 cup of the sweet and sour sauce. Cover tightly and place in the refrigerator until needed.*
2. *Arrange briquettes in the barbecue, lightly oil the grill rack, and preheat to high.*
3. *When ready, divide the turkey mixture into 4 or 6 equal pieces, form each piece into a ball, and flatten each ball to a thickness of 1/4 inch. Arrange on the grill rack 6 inches from the heat source, and cook for about 5 to 7 minutes. Flip the burgers, place a pineapple slice on each, and cook for an additional 5 to 6 minutes. Remove from the grill, and place on hamburger buns.*
4. *Meanwhile, in a saucepan, combine the remaining sweet and sour sauce and the crushed pineapple and cook over low until heated through. Transfer to a bowl, and serve alongside the burgers.*

To make honey soy sauce, see page 28.

Foil-Wrapped Cheeseburgers

6 servings

Vegetable oil, for the rack
2 pounds lean ground beef
Salt and pepper, to taste
1 (1-1/2 ounce) package dry onion soup mix
1/2 cup water
6 slices cheddar cheese
6 hamburger buns
Lettuce, for garnish

1. *Arrange charcoal in the barbecue and preheat to high. Clean and lightly oil the grill rack.*
2. *In a bowl, gently knead together the beef and salt and pepper to taste. (Be careful not to handle the meat too much or it will become tough.) Divide the mixture into 12 balls and flatten each ball into a 1/4-inch patty.*
3. *In a second bowl, stir together the soup and water until smooth. Place six 10-inch square pieces of aluminum foil on a flat surface. Lay a patty in the center of each foil square, brush with the soup mix, top with cheese, and then with a second patty. Press the edges of the patties together to seal them together. Brush with the remaining soup mixture and seal the edges of the foil together to create a pouch.*
4. *Arrange the pouches on the grill rack 4 inches from the heat source, and cook for 8 to 10 minutes per side, or until cooked as desired. Remove from the heat, transfer from the foil to the hamburger buns, garnish with lettuce, and serve.*

Spicy Sausage Burgers

4 servings

Vegetable oil, for the rack
1/2 pound lean ground beef
1/2 pound Italian sausage, casings removed
1/4 cup bottled hot sauce
4 slices provolone cheese
1/2 cup barbecue sauce, heated (see pages 122 to 124)

1. *Arrange briquettes in the barbecue, lightly oil the grill rack, and preheat to high.*
2. *In a bowl, gently knead the beef, sausage, and hot sauce. (Be careful not to handle the meat too much or it will become tough.) Divide into 4 equal pieces, form each piece into a ball, and flatten to a thickness of 1/4 inch.*
3. *When ready, arrange the burgers on the grill about 6 inches from the heat source, and cook, turning only once, for about 15 to 19 minutes. Just before removing from the heat, place a slice of cheese on each burger. When the cheese has melted, remove from the heat, and serve with barbecue sauce.*

The Hamburger: An Edible Icon

There is absolutely no other food that has taken a more prominent role in North American culture than the hamburger. The late journalist Charles Kuralt reported: "You can find your way across this country using burger joints the way a navigator uses stars. . . We have munched Bridge burgers in the shadow of the Brooklyn Bridge and Cable burgers hard by the Golden Gate, Dixie burgers in the sunny South and Yankee Doodle burgers in the North. . . We had a Capitol Burger—guess where. And so help us, in the inner courtyard of the Pentagon, a Penta burger."

An edible symbol, the burger sits on the throne of our culinary, and cultural, tradition. How it got there is the subject of much discourse, and even bitter disagreement in regards to some chapters of its history. Let's just take a quick glance at what is not disputed.

The oldest burger chain was established in 1921, when White Castle offered steam-fried burgers for a nickel apiece. Legend holds that long before White Castle, 18th century seamen in the large European port of Hamburg, Germany, had picked up a hankering for the raw, chopped beef they'd tasted while on their travels in Russia. By the time Germans came to America, the dish was transformed into a cooked version. No one knows for sure how it came to pass that beef patty met bun, or how lettuce, tomatoes, and onions joined the party. But today, billions of people throughout the world eat fried, steamed, and grilled varieties of this bounty of beef on a bun.

Garlicky Grilled T-Bone Steak

2 servings

2 T-bone steaks, 1-1/4-inches thick
1 tablespoon minced garlic
1 tablespoon snipped fresh basil
1 tablespoon minced fresh chives
1/3 cup extra virgin olive oil
Salt and pepper, to taste
Vegetable oil, for the rack

1. *Trim most but not all of the fat from the steaks, and place them in a zippered plastic bag.*
2. *In a cup, whisk together garlic, basil, chives, oil, and salt and pepper to taste. Pour into the plastic bag, seal, and shake to coat. Refrigerate for at least 3 to 5 hours.*
3. *Meanwhile, arrange the briquettes in the barbecue, clean and lightly oil the grill rack, and preheat to high.*
4. *Place the steak on the grill and cook, turning but not flipping, for about 5 to 7 minutes. Flip and cook for an additional 5 to 7 minutes, or until cooked as desired.*

Barbecued Beef Tenderloin

8 to 12 servings

Vegetable oil, for the rack
1 beef tenderloin, 4 to 6 pounds
1/4 cup melted butter
1/4 teaspoon bottled hot sauce

1. *Arrange the charcoal in the barbecue, clean and lightly oil the grill rack, and preheat to high.*
2. *Stir together the melted butter and hot sauce.*
3. *When ready, brush the tenderloin with the butter sauce and set on the grill about 4 inches from the heat source. Cook for about 18 to 27 minutes per side, basting with the butter sauce, or until cooked as desired. Remove from the grill, let settle, slice, and serve.*

Grilled Flank Steak with Celery Ketchup Marinade

About 6 servings

1 flank steak, 1-1/2 pounds
1 1/2 cups Celery Ketchup Marinade (see page 139)

1. *Place the steak in a shallow baking dish, cover with the marinade, and refrigerate, turning occasionally, 3 to 5 hours.*
2. *Remove from the refrigerator, and bring to room temperature. Place the marinade in a saucepan, bring to a boil, remove from the heat, and set aside.*
3. *Arrange a layer of charcoal in the barbecue and preheat to high. Adjust the grill rack to 4 inches from the heat source.*
4. *Place the steak on the grill rack and cook for 5 to 7 minutes. Flip and cook for an additional 5 to 7 minutes, or until cooked as desired. Remove from the heat, cut into thin slices, and serve with the marinade in a bowl on the side.*

Steak Dinner in Foil

About 2 servings

1 round steak, 12 ounces, cut into pieces
2 tablespoons flour
2 carrots, trimmed, pared, and cut into matchsticks
2 small white onions, peeled and quartered
2 small new potatoes, pared and sliced
1/2 medium green pepper, stemmed, seeded, and cut into rings
2 tablespoons ketchup
Salt and pepper, to taste
1 tablespoon water or white wine

1. *Place a 2-inch deep layer of charcoal in the barbecue, and preheat to high. Lay out two large squares of double thickness aluminum foil.*
2. *Dredge each steak in the flour, and pound using a meat mallet or the side of a knife. Place the steaks in the center of the foil, surround with the carrots, onion, potatoes, and bell pepper, top with the ketchup and salt and pepper to taste, and sprinkle with the water or white wine. Fold and seal the edges of the foil, place the packets on the grill, and cook for about 30 to 40 minutes, turning every 10 minutes or until cooked as desired.*
3. *Remove from the grill and serve.*

Marinating: A Flavor Bath for Your Food

Marinades have long been an effective method of enhancing the flavors of fish and meat. The right marinade can infuse a zesty zeal to any grill-bound goody. However, some marinades are powerful and may threaten to kill the meat's natural flavoring. A few simple suggestions will help you bring the perfect balance to your dinner plate.

- *To pack a full flavor punch, marinades really need to infuse the food— to help it along, pierce the meat all over with a fork or skewer prior to marinating.*
- *Generally, fish and other seafood require less than 45 minutes of soaking. After all, they've spent most of their lives marinating in the sea. To avoid tough seafood, use marinades with little or no acidic ingredients such as lemon, vinegar, and wine, which will cure the meat.*
- *Chicken is a tad more stubborn: Breasts take one hour of marinating, while thighs and wings may take up to two.*
- *If a thick cut of steak or lamb is cubed, soak the meat for three to five hours. If it's in one piece, let that baby bathe overnight. Remember, the larger the item, the longer its marinating time will require.*
- *More marinating methodology: If your meat is to steep for more than one hour, keep a lid on it. After marinating, meat should be drained and dried on a paper towel. Basting can be added after the meat begins cooking. Avoid aluminum containers for marinating because the acidic power of your marinade may corrode the metal and tarnish the flavor. And always refrigerate foods while they marinate.*

Barbecued Chuck Roast

6 to 8 servings

1 cup bottled barbecue sauce

3 tablespoons all-purpose flour

1 tablespoon packed dark brown sugar

1 medium beef chuck roast, about 3 pounds

2 stalks celery, roughly chopped

2 medium carrots, trimmed, pared, and roughly chopped

1 medium red onion, peeled and sliced

1. *Arrange the briquettes in the barbecue, set the grill rack about 6 inches from the heat source, and preheat to high*
2. *Lay out two sheets of aluminum foil measuring 30- x 18-inches, one on top of the other.*
3. *In a bowl, stir together the barbecue sauce, flour, and brown sugar until smooth and the sugar is dissolved. Spoon about 1/2 cup of sauce into the center of the double thickness of aluminum foil.*
4. *Place the roast on top of the sauce, add the celery, carrots, and onion, and drizzle the remaining sauce over the top. Pull up the sides of the foil, and seal with a double fold.*
5. *When ready, place the aluminum bundle on the barbecue, and cook, flipping only once, for about 1 to 1-1/2 hours, or until the meat is cooked as desired. Remove from the heat, slice, and serve immediately.*

Breaded Round Steak

10 to 12 servings

Vegetable oil, for the rack

1 large round steak, about 4 pounds, 1-1/2-inches thick

6 tablespoons butter or margarine, melted

1 tablespoon steak sauce

1 teaspoon mustard powder

1/2 teaspoon curry powder

1 cup fine dry bread crumbs

Salt and pepper, to taste

1. *Arrange the briquettes in a barbecue, clean and oil the grill rack, position it 5 to 6 inches from the heat source, and preheat to high.*
2. *Using a sharp knife, remove the fat from the steak.*
3. *In a small bowl, combine the butter, steak sauce, mustard powder, and curry powder.*
4. *When ready, place the steak on the preheated grill and cook, turning, for about 30 to 35 minutes, or until cooked as desired.*
5. *Remove the steak from the grill, and using a spatula, spread 1/2 of the butter mixture evenly over one side, and sprinkle with 1/2 of the bread crumbs. Repeat on the other side.*
6. *Return the steak to the grill and cook for about 5 to 8 minutes. Flip, and cook for another 5 to 8 minutes, or until the crumbs are a rich golden color. Remove from the grill, let rest for a few minutes, slice, and serve.*

Teriyaki Beef Kebabs

6 to 8 servings

1 small top round beef steak, about 2 pounds, 1-inch thick

1/4 cup packed light brown sugar

1/4 cup soy sauce

2 tablespoons fresh lime juice

1 tablespoon canola oil

1/4 teaspoon ginger powder

1 tablespoon minced garlic

Vegetable oil, for the rack and skewers

2-1/2 cups canned or fresh pineapple chunks

1. *Using a sharp knife, trim all the fat from the meat, and cut meat into 1-inch cubes.*
2. *In a bowl, stir together the sugar, soy sauce, lime juice, canola oil, ginger powder, and minced garlic until the sugar is dissolved. Add the meat, cover tightly, and refrigerate for about 8 hours, flipping occasionally.*
3. *When ready, arrange the briquettes in the barbecue, clean and lightly oil the grill rack, and preheat to high.*
4. *Thread the meat and pineapple, alternately, onto lightly oiled metal skewers. Immediately place on the barbecue, and cook, turning and basting with the marinade, for about 5 to 7 minutes, until the meat is cooked as desired. Remove from the heat and serve.*

Creative Kebabs

Kebabs have been used throughout the ages to grill meat quickly and easily. At a party, they are always a hit, especially when unusual items adorn these simple skewers. Try a raw veggie kebab with alternating hunks of broccoli, carrot, jicama, cherry tomatoes, and celery served with a bottled dressing or homemade dipping sauce. And keep in mind that these skewers don't always have to be savory. The fruit kabob never fails to please: Stack up a delicious, colorful array of fresh fruits like watermelon, pineapple, pear, grapes, and strawberries. Also, don't be afraid to mix and match—some great ideas, like banana and coconut shrimp kabobs, have made their way into the annals of gourmet history.

Barbecued Beef Short Ribs

6 to 8 servings

5 pounds short ribs
Vegetable oil, for the rack
1-1/2 cups ketchup
1/2 cup white wine vinegar
1/3 cup packed light brown sugar
1 tablespoon steak sauce
2 teaspoons grated lemon zest
1-1/2 teaspoons mustard powder
3/4 teaspoon garlic powder
Salt and pepper, to taste

1. *Place the ribs in a soup kettle or Dutch oven, cover with water, and bring to a boil. Reduce to a simmer, cover, and cook for about 1-1/2 to 2 hours, or until the meat on the ribs is fork tender. Transfer to a platter, and refrigerate for 3 to 5 hours.*
2. *About 30 minutes before needed, arrange briquettes in the barbecue, clean and lightly oil the grill rack, and preheat to high.*
3. *Meanwhile, in a bowl, stir together the ketchup, vinegar, sugar, steak sauce, lemon zest, mustard powder, garlic powder, and salt and pepper to taste.*
4. *Arrange the ribs on the preheated barbecue, and cook, turning and basting with the ketchup mixture, for about 20 minutes, or until heated through. Remove from the heat, and serve.*

Steak on the Coals

About 6 servings

1 sirloin steak, 3 pounds, 1-1/2- to 2-inches thick
1/2 cup cider vinegar
1/2 cup vegetable oil
1 small onion, peeled and minced
1 clove garlic, peeled and minced
1 teaspoon mustard powder
1/2 teaspoon nutmeg
1/4 teaspoon ground cloves
1/2 teaspoon bottled hot sauce

1. *Rinse the steak and cut away and discard any fat from the edge. Lay in a shallow, non-reactive baking pan.*
2. *In a blender or food processor, combine the vinegar, oil, onion, garlic, mustard powder, nutmeg, cloves, and hot sauce. Process on high until smooth and pour over the steak. Cover lightly and chill in the coldest part of the refrigerator, turning occasionally, for about 3 hours.*
3. *Remove the steak from the refrigerator, and allow to come to room temperature.*
4. *Meanwhile, place a 3-inch-deep layer of charcoal in the barbecue, and preheat to white-hot.*
5. *When ready, place the steak directly on the hot coals, and turn every ten minutes or so, moving the steak to another section of the charcoal that is white-hot. Allow the meat to cook for about 12 to 15 minutes per side for rare, or until cooked as desired. Remove from the charcoal, cut into serving-size pieces, and serve.*

Grilled Apple-Glazed Lamb Chops

4 to 8 servings

Vegetable oil, for the rack
1/2 cup apple jelly
1/4 cup lemon juice concentrate
1/4 cup steak sauce
8 loin lamb chops, 1-inch thick
Salt and pepper, to taste

1. *Arrange briquettes in the barbecue, clean and oil the grill rack, and preheat to high.*
2. *Meanwhile, in a small bowl, using a wire whisk, beat together the apple jelly, lemon juice, and steak sauce until smooth.*
3. *When ready, arrange the chops on the hot grill rack about 4 to 6 inches from the heat source and brush liberally with the glaze. Cook for about 10 to 12 minutes per side, basting with the glaze, until cooked as desired.*
4. *Transfer to a platter, season with salt and pepper, and serve with any remaining glaze in a bowl on the side.*

Barbecued Lamb Patties

About 4 servings

Vegetable oil, for the rack and basting
1/4 cup minced yellow onion
1/2 tablespoon minced garlic
3/4 pound lean ground lamb
1/4 pound lean ground beef or pork
1/4 teaspoon crushed dried basil
1/4 teaspoon crushed dried thyme
Salt and pepper, to taste

1. *Arrange briquettes in the barbecue, clean and oil the grill rack, and preheat to high.*
2. *In a bowl, combine the onion, garlic, lamb, beef, basil, thyme, and salt and pepper to taste. Cover tightly and refrigerate until the grill is ready.*
3. *When ready, divide the lamb mix into four equal portions, roll each into a ball, and flatten the balls into patties 1/2 inch thick.*
4. *Arrange the patties on the grill, brush with vegetable oil, and cook, flipping once, for about 7 to 10 minutes or until no longer pink and juices run clear. Serve with crusty bread.*

Lamb Kebabs

About 4 servings

Vegetable oil, for the rack and the skewers
About 1-1/2 cups Kebab Marinade (see page 140)
1 pound boneless lamb shoulder, cut into 1-inch pieces
2 cups cherry tomatoes
2 cups mushrooms, stems trimmed
1 large red bell pepper, stemmed, seeded,
    and cut into 1-inch squares
1 large yellow bell pepper, stemmed, seeded,
    and cut into 1-inch squares
8 large cloves garlic, unpeeled
Handful mint leaves, rinsed and patted dry
1 cup apple juice
2 or 3 tablespoons bottled fruit chutney
Raita, for serving (see page 133)

1. *Place the lamb in a bowl, add the marinade, cover tightly, and refrigerate for 4 to 5 hours.*
2. *When ready, arrange briquettes in the barbecue, clean and oil the grill rack, and preheat to high. Lightly oil four 8-inch skewers.*
3. *Drain the lamb, reserving the marinade. Thread the lamb, vegetables, mint, and garlic cloves alternately on the skewers, and place on the grill rack. Cook, turning and brushing with the marinade, for about 6 to 10 minutes, or until cooked as desired.*
4. *Pour any remaining marinade into a saucepan, add the apple juice and chutney, and bring to a boil. Reduce to a simmer, cover lightly, and cook, stirring occasionally, for about 5 minutes.*
5. *When ready, remove the kebabs from the grill, and serve with the Raita and the chutney sauce in a bowl on the side.*

Coney Island Hot Dogs

6 servings

6 hot dogs
Butter, for the hot dog buns
6 hot dog buns, sliced partway
About 6 tablespoons bottled hot sauce

1. *Cut the hot dogs in half diagonally without cutting through. Lay on the grill rack of a preheated barbecue about 4 inches from the heat source, and cook, turning, until plump and lightly browned.*
2. *Just before the hot dogs are done, butter each bun and place on the grill cut-side down. Heat for a moment but do not toast.*
3. *Spoon a tablespoon of the hot sauce onto each bun, place the hot dog in the bun, and serve.*

Jimmy's Chili Cheese Dogs

6 servings

6 hot dogs
6 hot dog buns, split partway
6 slices American or cheddar cheese
1 cup Chili con Carne (see page 158)
1 small onion, chopped

1. *Place the hot dogs on a hot grill and cook, turning, until plump and slightly charred.*
2. *Meanwhile, place the hot dog buns, cut-side down, over a smoldering section of the grill. Toast for 3 to 4 minutes, until slightly brown.*
3. *On sturdy plates, place the cooked hot dogs in the buns, and top each with a slice of cheese. Smother each hot dog with heaping spoonfuls of the chili, sprinkle with the chopped onion, and serve immediately.*

Dog Day Afternoon

The hot dog's history is as hazy as the steam surrounding New York City's famous frank carts. Accounts of its beginnings range dramatically, and include citations that date back to the 9th century B.C. to Homer's description of a man roasting sausage in *The Odyssey*. Frankfurt, Germany, is happy to take credit for the invention of the frankfurter—in 1987, the city celebrated the 500th birthday of the hot dog, putting its date of birth in 1487. Others claim that a butcher from another German town, Coburg, developed the "daschund" or "little dog" sausage and later promoted it in Frankfurt. The people of Vienna (Wien), Austria, point to the term "wiener" to stake their claim to the birthplace of the hot dog. Still, the wiener needs a bun to be a hot dog. How that metamorphosis took place remains something of a mystery. By 1916, the market for hot dogs—with buns— appeared to be lucrative to one Nathan Handwerker. He opened a hot dog stand in Coney Island, New York, the first in an empire now known as Nathan's Famous, Inc.

Whatever questions swirl around frankfurter history—When and why was it first served on a bun? Did it originate in Germany or Austria?—there is no doubt that the little dog has taken its place on our plates.

Grilled Sausage

4 servings

Vegetable oil, for the rack
1/4 cup honey mustard
1 teaspoon cider vinegar
1 large egg yolk
1 tablespoon snipped fresh dill
1-1/2 pounds sausage of choice

1. *Arrange briquettes in the barbecue, clean and oil the grill rack, and preheat to high.*
2. *In a saucepan, combine the honey mustard, vinegar, egg yolk, and dill. Cook over low heat, stirring, until thickened. Remove from the heat, stir in the dill, and let cool.*
3. *Using the point of a sharp knife, pierce the sausages several times, then arrange them on the hot grill rack about 4 to 6 inches from the heat source. Cook for about 8 to 12 minutes, turning, or until lightly browned.*
4. *Remove the sausages from the heat, cut into serving-size pieces, and serve with the mustard dip on the side.*

Grilled Ham Steak with Orange-Spice Glaze

About 6 servings

Vegetable oil, for the rack
1-1/2 cups frozen orange juice concentrate, thawed
1/2 cup cider vinegar
1/4 cup packed light brown sugar
2 teaspoons ground cloves
1 teaspoon mustard powder
1 teaspoon ginger powder
1 tablespoon molasses
1 tablespoon white wine or water
1 ham steak, about 1-1/2 to 2 pounds, 1-inch thick

1. *Arrange charcoal in the barbecue, and clean and lightly oil the grill rack.*
2. *In a blender or food processor, combine the orange juice, vinegar, sugar, cloves, mustard powder, ginger powder, molasses, and wine. Process on high until the sugar is dissolved and the sauce is smooth.*
3. *Place the ham steak on the grill, brush with the sauce, and cook for about 5 to 7 minutes per side, brushing frequently with the sauce, until the steak is a rich, deep brown. Remove from the heat, slice, and serve with the remaining sauce on the side.*

Grilled Pork Chops with Allspice and Thyme

About 6 servings

Vegetable oil, for the rack
1/2 teaspoon snipped fresh thyme leaves
1/4 teaspoon ground allspice
Salt and pepper, to taste
6 pork chops, 1-inch thick

1. *Arrange briquettes in the barbecue, clean and lightly oil the grill rack, and preheat to high.*
2. *In a bowl, combine the thyme, allspice, and salt and pepper to taste. Vigorously rub the mixture on both sides of each pork chop, and set aside until ready to cook.*
3. *When ready, arrange the pork chops on the hot grill about 6 inches from the heat source, and cook, flipping once, for about 8 to 14 minutes, or until the chops are cooked to an internal temperature of 160° F and juices run clear.*

Basil or tarragon can also be added or substituted for the thyme.

A Day at the Races

Long live the age-old relay! At your next backyard barbecue, designate teams and try on some of these favorite relay races for size:

- **EGG ON A SPOON:** *At different stations, racing team members must pass an uncooked egg—ever so delicately, but quickly—from spoon to spoon. Break the egg and you're out. The first team to cross the finish line with an unbroken egg wins.*

- **ORANGE UNDER THE CHIN:** *There may be no threat of breakage with this race, but be prepared to get close with your teammates. The orange is carried under the chin of the racer and passed to teammates chin to chin. No hands!*

- **THREE-LEGGED RACE:** *Buddy up with a teammate 'cause you'll almost be walking in his shoes for this one. Partners stand side by side. Use a towel, rag, or bandana to tie your inside foot at the ankle with your partner's inside foot. Whichever team crosses a designated line and then returns to a starting line first is the three-legged winner.*

- **CRAB-WALKING RACE:** *Sit down, put your hands behind your back and raise your torso. This is the position for the crab-walking race, which can be conducted forwards and backwards.*

- **POTATO-SACK RACE:** *Bust out the burlap for this one. If the burlap isn't available, an old pillowcase should suffice. Put your legs inside and hop along toward glory.*

Quickie Chicken

About 6 servings

3 whole boneless, skinless chicken breasts
Lightly salted water, to cover
Vegetable oil, for the rack
Barbecue sauce of choice (see pages 122 to 124)

1. *Using a sharp knife, cut away any fatty deposits from the chicken breasts, and place the breasts in a saucepan or soup kettle. Add enough water to cover, bring to a boil, and cook, skimming the scum from the water, for about 15 minutes.*
2. *Remove the chicken from the heat, drain, and let cool slightly. Wrap each breast in plastic wrap, or place in a zippered plastic bag, date, and place in the freezer until needed.*
3. *When needed, remove the chicken from the freezer, unwrap, and thaw for about 15 to 20 minutes.*
4. *Meanwhile, arrange briquettes in the barbecue, clean and lightly oil the grill rack, position it about 6 inches from heat source, and preheat to high.*
5. *Arrange the chicken breasts on the grill rack, brush liberally with barbecue sauce, and heat through, turning and basting, for about 10 minutes. Remove from heat, slice, and serve.*

Golden Chicken

4 to 6 servings

Vegetable oil, for the rack
1 medium whole chicken, about 3 pounds
2 teaspoons La Gènte seasoning (see page 117)
1/2 teaspoon crushed dried rosemary
1/2 teaspoon grated lemon zest
1/2 teaspoon paprika
1/4 cup sweet vermouth
1/4 cup extra virgin olive oil

1. *Arrange briquettes in the barbecue, position the grill rack 6 inches from the heat source, brush lightly with oil, and preheat to high.*
2. *Thoroughly wash the chicken under running water, and pat dry using paper towels. Rub the interior of the chicken with 1 teaspoon of La Gènte seasoning. Truss and tie the chicken, and secure tightly on a spit.*
3. *In a bowl, whisk together the remaining La Gènte seasoning, rosemary, lemon zest, paprika, vermouth, and olive oil until smooth.*
4. *Place the chicken over the coals, engage the motor of the spit, and cook, basting frequently with the herb sauce, for about 40 to 55 minutes, or until the juice of the chicken runs clear. Remove from the barbecue, carve, and serve immediately.*

If you don't have a spit, you can use this recipe with quartered chicken.

Chicken Pueblo

4 to 6 servings

2 small broiling chickens, 2–3 pounds, halved (see Box, page 98)
1 (8 ounce) can tomato sauce
1/4 cup extra virgin olive oil
1 tablespoon finely chopped jalapeño peppers
1/4 cup red wine vinegar
1 teaspoon onion powder
1 teaspoon garlic powder
Vegetable oil, for the rack
1/2 cup grated sharp cheddar cheese (optional)
Lime wedges, for serving

1. *Thoroughly wash the chicken under running water, pat dry using paper towels, and place in a roasting pan.*
2. *In a blender or food processor, combine the tomato sauce, olive oil, jalapeño peppers, vinegar, onion powder, and garlic powder and process until smooth. Pour over the chicken and rub in until all parts are coated. Cover and refrigerate for at least 8 hours.*
3. *Arrange briquettes in the barbecue, position the grill rack 6 inches from the heat source, brush lightly with oil, and preheat to high. Remove the chicken from the refrigerator and bring to room temperature.*
4. *Arrange the chicken on the grill rack, and cook, basting with the remaining marinade, for about 40 minutes, or until deep golden brown on all sides, and the juices run clear. If cheese is desired, five minutes before removing the chicken from the heat, arrange it skin-side up, sprinkle with the cheese, and allow it to melt. Remove from the heat and cut into serving-size pieces. Garnish with lime wedges and serve.*

Mediterranean Grilled Chicken

6 to 8 servings

2 large broiling chickens, 4–5 pounds, halved (see Box, page 98)

1/2 cup extra virgin olive oil

1/2 cup dry white wine

1/4 cup honey

1/4 cup white wine vinegar

2 teaspoons garlic powder

1 teaspoon La Gènte seasoning (see page 117)

1/2 teaspoon crushed dried oregano

1 large lemon, thinly sliced

1 large orange, thinly sliced

Vegetable oil, for the rack

Small handful fresh oregano leaves, rinsed, patted dry,
  and chopped

1. *Thoroughly wash the chicken under running water and pat dry using paper towels. Place in a zippered plastic bag.*
2. *In a blender or food processor, combine the olive oil, wine, honey, vinegar, garlic powder, La Gènte seasoning, and oregano, and process on low until smooth. Pour over the chicken, add the lemon and orange slices, seal the bag, and shake briefly to coat. Refrigerate for at least 8 hours.*
3. *Arrange briquettes in the barbecue, position the grill rack 6 inches from the heat source, brush lightly with oil, and preheat to high. Remove the chicken from the refrigerator and bring to room temperature. Sprinkle with the oregano leaves.*
4. *Arrange the chicken on the grill rack, and cook, basting with the remaining marinade, for about 40 minutes, or until deep golden brown on all sides, and the juices run clear. Remove from the heat, and serve immediately.*

To Halve or Halve Not: Splitting a Chicken

Why did the chicken cross the road? Not necessarily to be split in two beneath the wheels of a semi, one can presume. That work is done in the kitchen.

To halve—or "butterfly"—chickens, Cornish hens, and other game birds, you need to split the bird in half and open flat like a book, so it looks a little like the spread wings of a butterfly. A heavy knife or poultry scissors work best. Place the bird breast down. Cut through the rib cage along one side of the backbone, moving from tail to neck. Repeat on the other side of the spine to remove the backbone. Turn the bird breast-side up. Flatten the breast with the heel of your hand with enough pressure to break the breastbone. Fold the wing tips behind the shoulders before threading a long skewer through one wing, the top of the breast, and out through the other wing. Use a second skewer for pinning together the thighs and the bottom of the breast. The skewers will keep the bird flat during cooking and make it easier to turn over. Now that your chicken is halved, you can continue with your recipe as directed.

Chicken Teriyaki

4 servings

4 large boneless, skinless chicken breasts
1/4 cup soy sauce
1/4 cup extra virgin olive oil
1/2 cup dry sherry or white port wine
1-1/2 teaspoons garlic powder
1/2 teaspoon ginger powder
1 (10 ounce) jar kumquats
2 medium limes, cut into 8 wedges
Vegetable oil, for the rack and skewers

1. *Thoroughly wash the chicken under running water and pat dry using paper towels. Using a sharp knife, cut into 16 narrow strips, lengthwise. Place the strips in a zippered plastic bag.*
2. *In a blender, combine the soy sauce, olive oil, sherry, garlic powder, ginger powder, and process on low until smooth. Pour over the chicken, seal the bag, shake briefly, and refrigerate for at least 8 hours.*
3. *Arrange briquettes in the barbecue, position the grill rack 6 inches from the heat source, brush lightly with oil, and preheat to high. Remove the chicken from the refrigerator and bring to room temperature. Meanwhile, lightly grease 8 metal skewers.*
4. *Thread one end of a piece of chicken on a prepared skewer, then thread on a kumquat, the other end of the chicken strip, a lime slice, another chicken strip and kumquat, and the end of the second chicken strip. Repeat until all the chicken, kumquats, and limes are used.*
5. *Arrange the chicken on the grill rack and cook, basting with the remaining marinade, for about 15 minutes. Remove from the heat and serve immediately.*

Beer-Glazed Grilled Turkey Drumsticks

About 4 servings

Vegetable oil, for the rack
4 small turkey or large chicken drumsticks
1-1/2 cups beer or ale, 1/4 cup reserved
6 cups water
1 medium yellow onion, peeled and sliced
3/4 cup bottled hot sauce
1 teaspoon mustard powder

1. *Arrange briquettes in the barbecue, clean and lightly oil the grill rack, and preheat to high.*
2. *In a soup kettle or Dutch oven, combine the drumsticks, 1-1/4 cups of the beer, the water, and the onion. Bring to a boil, reduce to a simmer, cover, and cook for about 30 minutes. Remove from the heat.*
3. *Meanwhile, in a bowl, whisk together the hot sauce, the remaining 1/4 cup beer, and the mustard powder.*
4. *When the drumsticks are ready, transfer them to the barbecue and cook, turning and basting with the sauce for about 30 minutes, or until fork tender and the juices run clear. Remove from the heat.*
5. *Place any remaining sauce in a saucepan, bring to a boil, remove from the heat, and serve alongside the drumsticks.*

Indonesian Chicken Saté

4 to 6 Servings

2 small broiling chickens, 2–3 pounds, quartered
1/2 cup lite soy sauce
1/2 cup creamy peanut butter
1/4 cup dry sherry or white port wine
1/4 cup safflower oil
2 tablespoons molasses
1 tablespoon curry powder
1 teaspoon garlic powder
1 teaspoon grated lime zest
1/4 cup fresh lime juice
1 lemon, sliced
1 orange, sliced
Vegetable oil, for the rack

1. *Thoroughly wash the chicken under running water and pat dry using paper towels. Place in a zippered plastic bag.*
2. *In a blender, combine the soy sauce, peanut butter, sherry, safflower oil, molasses, curry powder, garlic powder, lime zest, and lime juice and process on low until smooth. Pour over the chicken, add the lemon and orange slices, seal the bag, and shake briefly. Refrigerate for at least 8 hours.*
3. *Arrange briquettes in the barbecue, position the grill rack 6 inches from the heat source, brush lightly with oil, and preheat. Remove the chicken from the refrigerator and bring to room temperature.*
4. *Arrange the chicken on the grill rack and cook, basting with the remaining marinade, for about 40 minutes, or until a deep golden brown on all sides and juices run clear. Remove from the heat, and serve immediately.*

Provençal Chicken Burgers

4 to 6 servings

1 pound ground chicken or turkey
1/8 cup finely chopped zucchini
1 tablespoon snipped fresh tarragon leaves
1 tablespoon minced white onion
1 tablespoon sour cream or plain yogurt
Salt and pepper, to taste
Vegetable oil, for the rack
Barbecue Sauce (see pages 122 to 124)

1. *In a large bowl, gently knead together the chicken, zucchini, tarragon, onion, sour cream, and salt and pepper to taste. Cover tightly and chill in the refrigerator until needed.*
2. *Arrange the briquettes in the barbecue, clean and lightly oil the grill rack, and preheat to high.*
3. *When ready, divide the chilled meat into 4 or 6 equal pieces, form each piece into a ball, and flatten to a thickness of 1/4 inch. Arrange on the grill rack about 6 inches from the heat source, and cook for about 5 to 7 minutes. Flip and continue to cook for about 5 minutes, or until no longer pink. Remove from the heat and serve immediately with barbecue sauce on the side.*

Grilled Salmon Steaks with Lemon-Herb Rub

About 4 servings

1 large salmon steak, 1 pound, 1-inch thick
Lemon-Herb Rub (see page 121)
Vegetable oil, for the rack

1. *Rub the steak with the Lemon-Herb Rub, cover, and place in the refrigerator for 30 minutes.*
2. *Arrange the briquettes in the barbecue, clean and oil the grill rack, and preheat to high.*
3. *When ready, place the steak on the grill, about 6 inches from the heat source, and cook for about 5 minutes, basting with the marinade. Turn, and continue to cook for about 5 minutes, basting, until the fish flakes easily when pierced with a fork. Remove from the heat, quarter, and serve with a compound butter on the side (see page 171).*

Fishing for Fresh Ones: Buying Fresh Fish

For the novice angler, hooking a fish can be a challenging endeavor. Likewise, for the grocery shopper who may not know the ins and outs of the fish department, selecting fresh fish can be a challenge. At reputable markets, lower prices can be reliable indicators that fish are fresh, in season, and plentiful. Also, closely examine the fish: The flesh should stick firmly to the bone; and it should smell of the sea, but without offensively pungent odors. When you bring your fish home, rinse it in cold water. Fresh fish is usually available in markets in these forms: Whole round–the eyes should be clear, the gills red, and the skin shiny, with tightly clinging scales; dressed–with scales or entrails removed; steaks–widthwise cuts of larger fish that are ready to cook; and Filets–ready-to-cook lengthwise cuts.

Grilled Shrimp Scampi

6 servings

1-1/2 pounds shrimp, rinsed, patted dry, shelled, and deveined

1/4 cup extra virgin olive oil

1/4 cup fresh lemon juice

3 tablespoons snipped fresh parsley

1 tablespoon minced garlic

Salt and pepper, to taste

1/4 teaspoon red pepper flakes

Vegetable oil, for the rack

1. *Thread the shrimp onto skewers and place them in a non-reactive baking dish.*
2. *In a medium non-reactive bowl, whisk together the olive oil, lemon juice, parsley, garlic, salt and pepper to taste, and red pepper flakes until incorporated. Pour the marinade over the shrimp to coat. Cover the baking dish and place in the refrigerator for 30 minutes.*
3. *Preheat the grill to high, and lightly oil the rack.*
4. *Remove the shrimp skewers from the marinade and place on the grill. Cook for 2 to 3 minutes per side, turning with tongs. When done, remove the shrimp from the skewers and serve with pasta or rice.*

Baja Fish Tacos

6 servings

1 pound cod filets or other white fish

2 tablespoons canola oil

1/4 cup chopped fresh cilantro

1 clove garlic, minced

Salt and pepper, to taste

Vegetable oil, for the rack

6 soft corn tortillas

1 lime, cut into 6 wedges

Shredded cabbage, for serving

Chopped tomato, for serving

Guacamole, for serving (see page 36)

Pico de Gallo, for serving (see page 129)

1. *Place the cod filets in a non-reactive bowl or baking dish. In a medium bowl, whisk together the canola oil, cilantro, garlic, and salt and pepper to taste and rub all over the cod filets. Cover and marinate in the refrigerator for 30 minutes to 1 hour.*
2. *Meanwhile, preheat the grill to high and oil the rack well.*
3. *Place the cod filets in fish baskets or on a fish grate, if available, and place on the grill. (If using a fish basket or grate, oil it well before cooking the fish. If grilling the fish directly on the rack, spray the filets themselves with cooking spray.) Cook the filets for about 6 minutes or until fish flakes easily.*
4. *To assemble the tacos, divide the cod filets between the tortillas and squeeze a wedge of lime over each. Pile cabbage, tomato, Guacamole, and Pico de Gallo on each taco and serve, with sour cream on the side if desired.*

Sherry-Soy Seafood Kebabs with Mango-Ginger Salsa

About 6 servings

1 pound swordfish

1/2 pound shrimp, rinsed, patted dry, shelled, and deveined

1/2 pound sea scallops, rinsed, drained, and muscle removed

1/2 cup dry sherry

1/2 cup rice wine

1/4 cup soy sauce

1 tablespoon fresh lemon juice

1 medium clove garlic, peeled and minced

1/4 teaspoon ginger powder

6 tablespoons peanut oil

Vegetable oil, for the rack

Mango-Ginger Salsa, for serving (see page 129)

1. *Thoroughly rinse the fish under running water, and pat dry using paper towels. Use a sharp knife to cut away and discard skin or other unwanted sections, and cut into 1- x 1-1/2-inch pieces. Place in a bowl with the shrimp and scallops.*

2. *In a blender, combine the sherry, rice wine, soy sauce, lemon juice, garlic, ginger powder, and peanut oil. Process on high until smooth, and then pour over the seafood pieces in the bowl.*

3. *Cover tightly and refrigerate for about 1 hour.*

4. *Preheat grill or broiler to high and oil the rack well.*

5. *When ready, thread the seafood alternately onto metal or bamboo skewers, and cook, turning, for about 6 to 8 minutes, basting with the remaining marinade or until the fish flakes easily. Remove from the heat and serve with Mango-Ginger Salsa on the side.*

Grilled Prosciutto-Wrapped Sea Scallops

8 servings

Vegetable oil, for the rack

1/2 pound prosciutto, thinly sliced

2 pounds sea scallops, rinsed, drained, and muscle removed

Salt and pepper, to taste

1/2 cup extra virgin olive oil or melted butter

1. *Preheat grill to high and lightly oil the rack.*

2. *Cut the prosciutto into narrow strips and wrap a strip around the perimeter of each scallop. Secure with a toothpick and season with salt and pepper to taste (be careful not to use too much salt, as the prosciutto is salty).*

3. *Place the scallops on the hot grill and cook for 2 to 3 minutes per side, basting both sides with the olive oil. When the scallops are white and slightly firm, remove them from the heat and serve.*

A Great Game for the Great Outdoors

At your next barbecue, a large crowd with a lot of undirected energy can be a lot to handle. A relaxed pickup game of Ultimate Frisbee should get people pumped. This addictive sport is a combination of soccer, football, and Frisbee. A non-contact sport played by two seven-player teams, the object of the game is to score goals by getting the disc into a team-mate's hands in the "end zone." The disc may only travel downfield by passes—like in basketball, players can pivot but are prohibited from stepping with the disk. Any time a pass is incomplete, intercepted, knocked down, or contacts an out-of-bounds area, the possession of the disc changes teams.

The game can be played with any variation of the rules agreed upon by the captains of the two teams, including, for example, altering the dimensions of a playing field for the sake of necessity (i.e., your backyard may be punier than the regular playing field). There are dozens upon dozens of organized Ultimate Frisbee leagues across the globe—find one in your area for more game rules and tips. Whatever rules you choose, the game's sure to be a blast. As one of the "Ten Commandments of the Disc" proclaims, "the single most difficult move with a disc is to put it down."

Grilled Tofu Sandwiches with Red Onion-Cucumber Salsa

4 to 6 servings

1 tablespoon coriander seeds

1 tablespoon cumin seeds

1 tablespoon paprika

2 small red chile peppers, stemmed

1 piece fresh ginger root, about 1 inch

2 tablespoons turmeric powder

1 tablespoon garam masala

1 cup plus 3 tablespoons plain yogurt or sour cream, 1 cup reserved

3 (14 ounce) packages semi-firm tofu

2 tablespoons fresh lemon juice

1 medium red onion, peeled and sliced

2 tablespoons snipped fresh cilantro

1 small cucumber, peeled and sliced

Salt and pepper, to taste

4 pita breads

1. *In a blender, combine the coriander seeds, cumin seeds, paprika, chile peppers, ginger, turmeric, garam masala, and 3 tablespoons of the yogurt and process on high until smooth.*
2. *Drain the water from the tofu, and cut into 2- x 2-inch squares. Sprinkle with the lemon juice and place in a bowl. Pour the yogurt mixture over the tofu and refrigerate for at least 1 hour.*
3. *Preheat grill to high.*
4. *When ready, thread the tofu onto bamboo skewers, and grill until lightly browned on all sides.*
5. *Meanwhile, combine the onion, cilantro, cucumbers, and salt and pepper to taste.*
6. *Heat the pitas in a lightly greased skillet.*
7. *To serve, slice open the pitas, fill with the salsa, and top with a tofu skewer. Serve with the yogurt sauce in a bowl on the side.*

Bamboo skewers should be soaked in water for at least 30 minutes before placing on the grill to ensure that they don't burn.

Campfire Crooners

What better way to warm your spirits in the woods, or even in your backyard—if the neighbors don't mind—than belting out campfire songs? Beneath a symphony of stars, even the shyest among us will join in on an old favorite. Here are some better-known ditties to get you going:

"This Land Is Your Land"; "Comin' Round the Mountain"; "You Are My Sunshine"; "I'm an Old Cowhand (From the Rio Grande)"; "Mockingbird" "Get Along, Little Doggies"; "Puff the Magic Dragon"; "Free to Be You and Me"; "If I Had a Hammer"

And don't forget your favorite pop songs, show tunes, and kid-friendly classics. For some inspiration, check out a song list or two, which are available on the Internet or at a book or music store.

Grilled Tofu with Red and White Miso

4 to 6 servings

1 (14 ounce) package semi-firm tofu
1 tablespoon red miso paste
2 teaspoons white miso paste
2 large egg yolks
1/2 teaspoon granulated sugar
1/4 cup vegetable stock

1. *One hour before needed, drain the water from the tofu, wrap in a piece of cheesecloth, and set in a sieve, placing a small plate on top.*
2. *In the top of a double boiler, combine the red miso, white miso, egg yolks, sugar, and vegetable stock. Place over boiling water and cook, stirring until the mixture thickens. Remove from the heat.*
3. *When the tofu is ready, remove from the cheesecloth, and cut into 4 cubes. Carefully press two pieces onto one skewer, repeat with the second two pieces, and place on a preheated barbecue. Cook for about 2 to 3 minutes, or until the tofu is a speckled brown color. Spread with the miso sauce and serve immediately.*

Jenny's Favorite Tofu Burger

About 8 servings

1 medium yellow onion, peeled and finely chopped
2 (8 ounce) packages semi-firm tofu, crumbled
2 cups cold vegetable stock or water
1/2 cup fine dried breadcrumbs
2 tablespoons Worcestershire sauce
Pepper, to taste
8 multigrain rolls, for serving
Lettuce, tomatoes, and sliced mushrooms for serving

1. *In a saucepan, sauté the onion with a small amount of water until translucent.*
2. *Preheat grill to high.*
3. *In a bowl, knead together the sautéed onion, tofu, stock, breadcrumbs, Worcestershire sauce, and pepper to taste. Pinch off pieces and form into 8 patties.*
4. *Transfer the patties to the grill, and cook, flipping, for about 5 minutes per side. Remove from the heat and serve on the rolls with the lettuce, tomatoes, and mushrooms.*

Grilled Portabella & Parmesan Sandwiches with Pesto Sauce

4 servings

4 large portabella mushrooms, about 10 ounces each
1/2 cup Pesto Sauce (see page 137), divided
Salt and pepper, to taste
4 ciabatta or other crusty rolls
12 generous slices Parmesan cheese
Small bunch arugula, rinsed and patted dry
2 large tomatoes, stemmed and sliced

1. *Stem the mushrooms and wipe them clean with a moist cloth. Brush both sides of each mushroom with 1/4 cup of the Pesto Sauce (you can do this up to 3 hours before cooking, if you'd like to marinate the mushrooms). Season with salt and pepper, to taste.*
2. *Preheat grill to high.*
3. *When ready to cook, drain the Pesto Sauce from the mushrooms and place them stem-side down on the grill. Cook for about 3 minutes, then flip and cook 4 to 6 minutes more. Remove from the heat.*
4. *Slice open the rolls and brush with the remaining Pesto Sauce. Layer some arugula and tomatoes on each roll, top with a portabella and some Parmesan slices, and serve.*

Mykonos-Style Grilled Sliced Eggplant

6 to 8 servings

About 2 pounds slender eggplant

Sea salt, for sweating the eggplant

4 tablespoons extra virgin olive oil

1 medium green bell pepper, stemmed, seeded,
   and cut into matchsticks

3 medium tomatoes, peeled, seeded, and sliced

1/2 teaspoon crushed dried oregano

1-1/4 cup plain yogurt

1 tablespoon minced garlic

1/2 teaspoon crushed dried dill

1. *Using a sharp knife, trim the ends from the eggplant, slice into 1/2-inch thick slices, and sprinkle both sides of each slice with sea salt. Lay the eggplant on a wire rack covered with paper towels and cover with a second layer of paper towels. Weigh down with a plate and let drain for about 10 to 15 minutes. Preheat the grill to high.*
2. *Heat 3 tablespoons of the olive oil in a saucepan, and sauté the bell pepper, tomato, and oregano for 2 to 3 minutes.*
3. *Meanwhile, in a bowl, stir together the yogurt, garlic, and dill.*
4. *Thoroughly rinse the eggplant slices under running water, brush with the remaining oil, and cook on the grill for about 4 to 5 minutes. Turn 90 degrees in either direction and cook for an additional 3 minutes. Turn again and cook for 3 more minutes.*
5. *Remove from the grill, arrange on a serving platter, and spoon the pepper and tomatoes over the top. Serve immediately with the yogurt in a bowl on the side*

Rubs, Sauces & Marinades

A Day at the Beach

SIPS AND STARTERS

•

Honey Lemonade
Crunchy Cucumber Rounds
Vegetable Dip Verde

SALADS

•

Fresh Tomato Salad

ENTREES

•

Quickie Chicken
Grilled Portabella & Parmesan Sandwiches with Pesto Sauce

SIDES

•

Red & Green Slaw
Macaroni Salad

FROM THE BAKERY

•

World's Best Chocolate Chip Cookies

Milano Rub

About 1 cup

3 tablespoons crushed dried oregano

3 tablespoons crushed dried dill

3 tablespoons crushed dried lemon thyme

3 tablespoons crushed dried tarragon

3 tablespoons crushed dried rosemary

1 tablespoon crushed dried garlic flakes

Salt and pepper, to taste

In a food processor or spice or coffee grinder, combine the oregano, dill, lemon thyme, tarragon, rosemary, and garlic and process on low until blended, but not powdery. Add salt and pepper to taste and place in an airtight container.

Mary's Beef Rub

About 1-1/2 cups

1/4 cup packed dark brown sugar

1/4 cup paprika

3 tablespoons ground black pepper

1 tablespoon salt

2 teaspoons garlic powder

2 teaspoons onion powder

2 teaspoons red pepper flakes

2 teaspoons celery seeds

In a food processor or spice or coffee grinder, combine the sugar, paprika, black pepper, salt, garlic powder, onion powder, red pepper flakes, and celery seeds and process on high until smooth. Transfer to an airtight container.

Hickory Rub

About 2 tablespoons

2 teaspoons garlic salt

2 teaspoons onion salt

2 teaspoons hickory-flavored salt

2 teaspoons dried rosemary

1 teaspoon ground black pepper

1 teaspoon celery salt (optional)

In an airtight container, combine all the ingredients and use as a rub on beef or pork.

La Gènte Seasoning

About 1/2 cup

1 tablespoon ground cloves
1 tablespoon ground cinnamon
1 tablespoon crushed bay leaf
1 tablespoon ground allspice
2 tablespoons ground black pepper
1 tablespoon ground white pepper
2 teaspoons ground nutmeg
1 teaspoon celery seeds

In the container of a food processor or spice or coffee grinder, combine the cloves, cinnamon, bay leaf, allspice, black pepper, white pepper, nutmeg, and celery seeds and process on high until finely ground and powdery. Transfer to an airtight container and use as desired.

Because the ingredients are going to be ground, 1 teaspoon each of whole cloves and allspice can be substituted.

Zesty Seasoning

About 1/2 cup

1 tablespoon grated lemon zest
1 tablespoon ground mace or nutmeg
2 tablespoons ground cinnamon
1 tablespoon crushed dried basil
1 tablespoon crushed dried thyme
1 tablespoon crushed dried rosemary
1 tablespoon paprika
1/2 teaspoon ground black pepper
1 teaspoon ground cloves
1/2 teaspoon ground allspice
Salt, to taste

In a food processor or spice or coffee grinder, combine the lemon zest, mace, cinnamon, basil, thyme, rosemary, paprika, pepper, cloves, allspice, and salt to taste and process on low until blended. Transfer to an airtight container.

Spicy Dry Poultry Rub

About 1 cup

6 tablespoons salt

3 tablespoons ground black pepper

2 tablespoons garlic powder

1 tablespoon paprika

2 tablespoons mustard powder

2 tablespoons crushed dried bay leaves (optional)

In a jar or other container with a tight cover, combine the salt, pepper, garlic powder, paprika, mustard powder, and bay leaves and shake to blend.

Five Leaf Poultry Rub

About 2 tablespoons

1 teaspoon crushed dried sage

1 teaspoon crushed dried savory

1 teaspoon crushed dried parsley

1/2 teaspoon dried chives

1/2 teaspoon crushed dried basil

In a food processor or spice or coffee grinder, combine the sage, savory, parsley, chives, and basil and process on low until blended. Place in an airtight container.

Rub-a-dub-dub: How to Use Rubs

Tired of the same old meats you've been cooking for who knows how long? You don't necessarily need to hit the grocery store aisles hunting for new and better cuts of meat. With an effective spice rub, the solution to your blues may be sitting right in your own spice rack. Usually applied several hours before cooking, spice rubs are excellent for infusing flavor into meats that will be grilled, broiled, or baked. Lamb, pork, poultry, or beef—all will come alive with an effective rub. There are two variations of rubs: dry and wet. Dry rubs are merely concoctions of spices and herbs that are applied directly to the meat. To make a moist rub, stir in a dash of oil to make a thick paste and then smear generously over the uncooked meat. Wet rubs can help the seasoning adhere to the meat to create a flavorful crust. Both wet and dry rubs work similarly to marinades, and can be especially effective with barbecue-style cooking.

Eastern European Rub

About 1/4 cup

1 teaspoon crushed dried thyme

1/2 teaspoon onion powder

1 teaspoon garlic powder

1/2 teaspoon crushed dried marjoram

1/2 teaspoon crushed dried dill

1 teaspoon curry powder

1 tablespoon paprika

In a food processor or spice or coffee grinder combine the thyme, onion powder, garlic powder, marjoram, dill, curry powder, and paprika and process on low until blended. Transfer to an airtight container and use as desired on pork, beef, or lamb.

Kickin' Cayenne-Peppercorn Rub

About 1/2 cup

2 tablespoons cayenne pepper

1 tablespoon crushed black peppercorns

2 tablespoons onion powder

1 tablespoon garlic powder

2 teaspoons mustard powder

1 teaspoon crushed dried basil

1/2 teaspoons crushed dried cilantro

1 teaspoon paprika

1 teaspoon chervil

1-1/2 teaspoon celery seeds

1/4 teaspoon crushed dried sage

1/4 teaspoon ginger powder

Pinch lemon thyme

In a food processor or spice or coffee grinder, combine the ingredients and process on low until the peppercorns are ground and the mixture is thoroughly blended. Transfer to an airtight container and use as desired on poultry or pork.

Asian Rub

About 3/4 cup

2 whole star anise
2 tablespoons black peppercorns
1 tablespoon white peppercorns
1 tablespoon fennel seeds
1/2 teaspoon whole cloves
1/2 stick (about 1-1/2 inches) cinnamon
1/4 cup packed dark brown sugar
Salt and pepper, to taste

1. *In a microwave-proof container, combine all of the ingredients through the cinnamon and microwave on high for about 10 to 20 seconds or until the spices become fragrant. (Be careful not to overheat.)*
2. *In a food processor or a spice or coffee grinder, process the warm ingredients on high until finely ground.*
3. *In a bowl, combine the spices and brown sugar until smooth. Add salt and pepper to taste, and store in an airtight container.*

Greek Rub

About 1/4 cup

2 teaspoons salt (optional)
2 teaspoons crushed dried oregano
1-1/2 teaspoons onion powder
1-1/2 teaspoons garlic powder
1 teaspoon ground black pepper
1 teaspoon beef-flavored bouillon granules
1 teaspoon dried parsley
1 teaspoon crushed dried dill
1/2 teaspoon ground cinnamon
1/2 teaspoon ground nutmeg or mace

In a food processor or spice or coffee grinder, combine the salt, oregano, onion powder, garlic powder, black pepper, bouillon granules, parsley, dill, cinnamon, and nutmeg and process on low until blended. Place in an airtight container for use on lamb and fish.

Fine Herb Rub

About 1 cup

1 packed cup fresh chervil leaves
1/2 cup snipped fresh chives
1 packed cup fresh flat-leaf parsley leaves
1/2 cup snipped fresh tarragon leaves

1. *Thoroughly rinse the herbs under running water and pat dry using paper towels. Air dry on a wire rack covered with paper towels for at least 8 hours.*
2. *When ready, in a food processor or spice or coffee grinder, combine all of the herbs and process on low until blended. Place in a strainer over a bowl and let sit undisturbed for about 1 hour. The rub can be used fresh on any kind of meat, fish, or poultry or can be dried and stored for several months.*

Pilgrim's Progress Rub

About 4 tablespoons

1 tablespoon salt
1 tablespoon freshly ground black pepper
2 teaspoons crushed dried thyme
1 teaspoon crushed dried sage
1 teaspoon cayenne pepper
1 teaspoon onion powder
1 teaspoon garlic powder
1/2 teaspoon paprika

In a food processor or spice or coffee grinder, combine all the ingredients and process on low until blended. Transfer to an airtight container for use on turkey and other poultry.

Lemon Herb Rub

About 3/4 cup

4 tablespoons crushed dried basil
3 tablespoons crushed dried oregano
1 tablespoon ground black pepper
2 tablespoons granulated onion
1 tablespoon celery seeds
1 tablespoon crushed dried tarragon
1/2 teaspoon granulated garlic
1 tablespoon grated lemon zest

In a food processor or spice or coffee grinder, combine all of the ingredients and process on low until blended. Transfer to an airtight container for storage.

Classic Cookout Barbecue Sauce

About 3 cups

1/4 cup extra virgin olive oil
1/2 cup minced yellow onion
1/2 cup minced red or green bell peppers
3 tablespoons minced garlic
1 teaspoon red pepper flakes
2 cups tomato puree
1/3 cup packed dark brown sugar
Salt and pepper, to taste

1. *Heat the oil in a saucepan and sauté the onion, peppers, and garlic until the onion is golden. Add the red pepper flakes, tomato puree, and sugar. Cover tightly, and simmer over low heat for about 30 minutes.*
2 *Remove from the heat and add salt and pepper to taste. Use as a basting sauce for almost any type of meat or poultry. Sauce should be stored in the refrigerator.*

Zingy Carolina Barbecue Sauce

About 2-1/4 to 2-1/2 cups

2 tablespoons vegetable oil
1 medium yellow onion, peeled and coarsely chopped
1 medium clove garlic, peeled and coarsely chopped
2 tablespoons dark brown sugar
Pinch cayenne pepper
1 tablespoon mustard powder
1/2 cup chopped celery
1 tablespoon prepared horseradish
2 tablespoons rice wine vinegar
4 tablespoons fresh lime juice
1 cup tomato sauce
4 tablespoons Worcestershire sauce
1 cup apple juice

1. *Heat the oil in a saucepan and sauté the onion and garlic together until the onion is translucent. Stirring constantly, add the sugar, cayenne pepper, mustard powder, and celery. Heat through, and add the horseradish, vinegar, lime juice, tomato sauce, Worcestershire sauce, and apple juice. Bring to a boil and remove from the heat. Let cool slightly.*
2. *In a blender or food processor, puree the mixture in batches until smooth. Use as a marinade or basting sauce. Sauce should be stored in the refrigerator.*

Tangy Barbecue Sauce

About 2-1/4 to 2-1/2 cups

2 small yellow onions, peeled and chopped
1/2 cup tomato paste
1/2 cup vegetable oil
2 tablespoons diced celery
2 teaspoons mustard powder
2 teaspoons Worcestershire sauce
2 teaspoons fresh lemon juice
Salt and pepper, to taste

1. *In a saucepan, combine the onion, tomato paste, oil, celery, mustard powder, Worcestershire sauce, and fresh lemon juice and cook, stirring constantly, until the vegetables are tender.*
2. *Remove from the heat and puree in a blender or food processor until smooth. Add salt and pepper to taste and use as a marinade or basting sauce. Sauce should be stored in the refrigerator.*

No-Tomato Barbecue Sauce

1-3/4 cups

1/2 cup vegetable oil
1/2 cup fresh lemon juice
1/2 cup wine vinegar
1/4 cup soy sauce
1 teaspoon bottled hot sauce
Salt, to taste

In a medium bowl whisk together all ingredients and use to baste all meats and poultry. Sauce can be stored in the refrigerator for up to 3 weeks.

Bette's Barbecue Sauce

About 1-1/4 to 1-1/2 cups

1/4 cup melted butter
3/4 cup white wine
1 tablespoon minced garlic
1 large white onion, peeled and minced
1/4 teaspoon red pepper flakes
Pinch crushed dried tarragon
Pinch crushed dried French thyme
1 tablespoon snipped fresh basil
Salt and pepper, to taste

1. *In a blender or food processor, combine the butter, wine, garlic, onion, red pepper flakes, tarragon, thyme, and basil and process on high until smooth.*
2. *Place in a saucepan over medium heat and stir until bubbles form around the edge. Remove from the heat, add salt and pepper to taste, and use as a marinade or basting sauce. Sauce should be stored in the refrigerator.*

Venezuelan Guasacaca Barbecue Sauce

About 4 cups

1 cup minced onions
2 cloves garlic, minced
1 habañero pepper, seeded, stemmed, and minced
1 large ripe avocado, peeled, pitted, and chopped
2 cups peeled, seeded, and chopped tomatoes
1 cup extra virgin olive oil
1/4 cup red wine vinegar
1 teaspoon mustard
2 tablespoons minced Italian parsley
Salt, to taste

With a mortar and pestle, mash the onion, garlic, habañero pepper, avocado, and tomatoes into a paste. This may need to be done in batches. Transfer to a bowl and add the remaining ingredients, blending well with a fork. Guasacaca is delicious as a marinade or baste for shrimp, beef, or chicken.

Because this sauce contains fresh avocado, it should be used immediately.

Basic Steak Sauce

About 1 cup

1/2 cup butter or margarine
1/4 cup fresh lemon juice
1/4 cup Worcestershire sauce
1/4 teaspoon garlic powder
1/4 teaspoon onion powder

Melt the butter in a saucepan, add the fresh lemon juice, Worcestershire sauce, garlic and onion powders and bring to a boil. Remove from the heat, cool slightly, and use as a marinade or basting sauce.

Lemon Apple Glaze

4 to 6 servings

1/2 cup apple jelly
1/4 cup lemon juice concentrate
1/4 cup steak sauce

Combine the ingredients in a jar or cup and stir until well-integrated. Use to baste lamb while it is cooking.

Barbecue Glaze

About 1 cup

1/4 cup packed dark brown sugar
1 tablespoon cornstarch or arrowroot
2/3 cup apple juice
1/4 cup cider vinegar
1 teaspoon grated orange, lemon, or lime zest

In a saucepan, stir together the sugar and cornstarch until incorporated, then stir in the apple juice and vinegar. Bring to a boil, stirring constantly, until the sugar is dissolved. Reduce to a simmer, add the citrus zest, and cook, stirring, until thickened. Remove from the heat and use to brush on poultry, beef, pork, lamb, and sausage.

From the Pantry to the Fire Pit: Great, Simple Grilling Glazes

Plain pantry items no longer, your favorite jams, jellies, savories, and syrups can make meat transcendent on the grill. Some of these items may be used as a glaze straight from the jar, bottle, or can; others may need to be heated or mixed with a drop of hot water to thin them out. Once your glaze is slightly runny, simply brush it on the meat and slap the meat on the grill (and be sure to have some extra glaze on hand for basting). Here are some surefire favorites: apricot preserves, peach preserves, cherry preserves, orange marmalade, black currant jam or jelly, apple jelly, mango or ginger chutney, jellied cranberry sauce, maple syrup, light molasses, beer, ale, or stout, peanut butter or honey.

Cape Cod Glaze

About 3 cups

2 cups maple syrup
1/3 cup packed dark brown sugar
1 cup apple juice
1 cup cranberry juice
1 tablespoon finely grated lemon zest
1 tablespoon fresh orange juice
1/4 cup vegetable oil

1. *In a blender or food processor, combine the ingredients and process on high until very smooth and the sugar is dissolved.*
2. *Transfer to a saucepan over medium heat, and bring the mixture to a simmer. Cook, stirring, until thickened and reduced to about 3 cups (about 15 minutes). Remove from the heat, and use to baste poultry during the final 15 to 20 minutes of cooking time.*

Horseradish-Mustard Spread

About 1/3 cup

1 (3 ounce) package cream cheese, at room temperature
2 tablespoons sour cream
2 to 3 teaspoons prepared mustard
1/2 to 1 teaspoon prepared horseradish

In a blender or food processor, combine the cream cheese, sour cream, mustard, and horseradish and process on low until very smooth. Pour into a bowl, cover tightly and refrigerate for up to 3 weeks. Use as a spread on pork.

Herb Mustard Paste

About 1/4 cup

1 teaspoon Dijon or brown mustard
2 teaspoons butter or margarine
2 tablespoons snipped fresh parsley
2 tablespoons fresh lemon or lime juice

In a small bowl, using an electric mixer, beat together the mustard and butter until smooth. Beat in the parsley and fresh lemon juice. Slather on fish before cooking.

If you prefer, minced celery tops or snipped fresh basil can be substituted for the parsley.

Spicy Sweet & Sour Sauce

About 1-1/2 cups

1/4 cup firmly packed brown sugar

2 teaspoons cornstarch

1 cup water or apple juice

1/4 cup tomato ketchup

2 tablespoons vinegar

1 tablespoon Worcestershire sauce

About 3 drops bottled hot sauce, to taste

In a blender or food processor, combine the sugar, cornstarch, water, ketchup, vinegar, Worcestershire sauce, and hot sauce and process on high until smooth. Transfer to a saucepan, bring to a boil, and cook, stirring, until thick. Sauce should be stored in the refrigerator.

Great American Sweet and Sour Sauce

About 1/2 cup

2 tablespoons granulated sugar

1 tablespoon corn syrup

1/2 teaspoon chili powder

2/3 cups water

3 tablespoons ketchup

1 tablespoon cider vinegar

1/4 cup chopped sweet pickles

1. *In a blender or food processor, combine the sugar, corn syrup, chili powder, water, ketchup, and vinegar and process on high until smooth.*
2. *Pour into a saucepan, bring to a boil, reduce to a simmer, and cook for about 2 to 3 minutes. Remove from the heat, stir in the pickles, and use as a marinade or basting sauce. Sauce should be stored in the refrigerator.*

Dill Dipping Sauce

About 1 cup

1/2 cup sour cream
1/2 cup mayonnaise
2 tablespoons finely chopped dill pickle
1 teaspoon dried dill

In a blender or food processor, combine the sour cream, mayonnaise, dill pickle, and dill. Cover and refrigerate for at least 1 hour before serving with grilled fish, chicken, or vegetables.

Avocado Dipping Sauce

About 1-1/2 cups

1 (16 ounce) can chopped tomatoes
1 ripe avocado, peeled, pitted, and chopped
1/4 cup chopped green onion
1 (4 ounce) can chopped green chiles, drained
2 tablespoons white wine vinegar
1 tablespoon canola oil
Salt and pepper, to taste

In a bowl, using a hand mixer, blend together the tomatoes, avocado, onion, chiles, vinegar, oil, and salt and pepper to taste until smooth. Cover and refrigerate until needed.

The Quintessential Cooler

Whether you're off to the beach loaded down with beach paddleball accessories, sunscreen, bug repellant, chairs, and umbrellas, or you're on your way to a tailgate party to cheer on your favorite team, a well-stocked cooler represents a vital component to any successful outdoor outing. To get the most from your cooler, be sure to pack it wisely. Canned beverages, packages of hot dogs, and baggies of watermelon wedges are ideal for storing in your mobile mini-fridge. Peelable fruits that are easy to handle such as oranges and bananas are choice snacks when beach breezes threaten to sprinkle sand on your edibles. Just in case, toss in a cloth towel to wipe off items. The right-sized Tupperware can provide a perfect way to keep sandwiches, coleslaw, or potato salad from getting crushed. Pack canned, heavy, or larger items on the bottom after layering with ice. Arrange the contents in an orderly fashion, pile on more ice, and you and your cooler are good to go.

Mango-Ginger Salsa

About 3 cups

2 ripe mangoes, peeled, pitted, and diced
1 jalapeño pepper, stemmed, seeded, and chopped
1 red bell pepper, stemmed, seeded, and finely chopped
1 red onion, finely diced
1/2 cup chopped fresh cilantro
2 limes, juiced
1 medium piece ginger root (about 4 inches), peeled
Salt and pepper, to taste

1. *In a medium bowl, toss together the mango, jalapeño, bell pepper, onion, and cilantro with the lime juice.*
2. *Over a small bowl, grate the ginger as finely as possible. Scoop the grated ginger into a ball, collecting as much of the juice as possible, and squeeze over the bowl of salsa to extract the juice. Discard the squeezed ginger.*
3. *Toss the salsa with the ginger juice, add salt and pepper to taste, and serve. This sauce can be stored, covered, in the refrigerator for up to 3 days.*

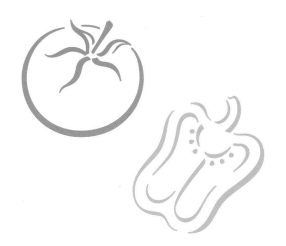

Pico de Gallo

About 2 cups

1-1/2 cups seeded, diced tomatoes
1/4 cup diced red onion
1 jalapeño pepper, stemmed and diced (remove seeds for a milder result)
1 clove garlic, minced
3 tablespoons chopped fresh cilantro
2 limes, juiced
1-1/2 tablespoons olive oil
Salt and pepper, to taste

Combine the tomatoes, onion, jalapeño, garlic, and cilantro in a bowl and toss with the lime juice and olive oil. Add salt and pepper to taste. Store, covered, in the refrigerator for up to 1 week.

Green Salsa

About 1-1/4 cups

Green Tomatoes: A Ripening Southern Tradition

Y ou say "tomato," I say "green tomato, y'all." Green tomatoes are considered a peculiarity of Southern cooking, but these pre-ripened delicacies are gaining fans fast across the land. Unlike their ripened red cousins, green tomatoes are not typically used in salads. Many recipes call for the fruit to be pickled or fried. For the fried variation, you can use breadcrumbs, cornmeal, flour, or even a coating of beaten eggs to give them a crust. In case you don't have home-grown tomatoes, a few things to keep in mind when selecting: Look for firm fruit with subtle aromas. Avoid any tomatoes with white specks that indicate they've been forced to ripen with gas. Also, fresh green tomatoes are good to keep in freezer bags because they should retain their flavor for extensive periods.

3 cups chopped green tomatoes
2 tablespoons chopped yellow onion
2 tablespoons minced garlic
2 tablespoons snipped fresh cilantro
2 small green chile peppers, stemmed, seeded, and sliced
Salt and pepper, to taste

Place the ingredients in a saucepan, bring to a boil, reduce to a simmer, and cook until the tomatoes are fork tender. Transfer to a food processor (a blender is not recommended) and process briefly on low to break up larger vegetable pieces. Transfer to a bowl, add salt and pepper to taste, and serve.

Mint Sauce

About 1 cup

1/2 cup cider vinegar

1/4 cup confectioners' sugar

1/4 cup fresh mint leaves, rinsed and patted dry

1. *In a saucepan, combine the vinegar and sugar and heat through, stirring constantly to remove any lumps, until the sugar is dissolved.*
2. *Place the mint in a bowl, pour the hot vinegar mixture over it, and set aside for one hour before using.*

Mustard Sauce

About 1-3/4 cups

1 cup evaporated milk

1/4 cup granulated sugar

2 tablespoons mustard powder

1 tablespoon cornstarch or arrowroot

1 large egg yolk

1/4 cup cider vinegar, heated

1. *Heat 3/4 cup of the evaporated milk over low heat.*
2. *In a cup, stir together the sugar, mustard powder, and cornstarch.*
3. *In a bowl, using a wire whisk, beat the egg yolk until foamy. Add the dry ingredients, and stir into the heated milk. Cook, stirring constantly, until the mixture starts to thicken. Remove from the heat and stir in the hot vinegar. Cool slightly before serving.*

Fun Under the Sun

Remember how great it was going to the beach when you were a kid? Let your inner child out to play—maybe even with your other children—on your next outing to the ocean. Bring games! Frisbees and tennis balls are essential for those games of catch in the ocean, or to keep the dog in check. For more organized beach games, consider the following:

KADIMA: You swing a paddle at a ball, hit the ball to your partner, and your partner hits it back, all the while trying to keep the ball from hitting the ground. This is a fun little game to play at the water's edge, because when the ball does fall, another game of trying to fish it from the frothy tide begins.

HACKEYSACK: This is probably the most convenient pouch of fun under the sun. A small leather or knitted sack filled with beads of plastic or other squishy material, the Hackeysack has been known to inspire people to stand around in circles lifting their legs or feet into strange positions. These folks are bent on keeping the ball in the air without using their hands. For such cheap entertainment, it's definitely worth looking into, if only to keep the kids busy while you're catching some rays.

Volleyball and horseshoes are other good beach bets.

Raita

About 2-1/2 cups

1 medium (about 5 inches) cucumber, trimmed, peeled, and grated
1/2 teaspoon coarse salt
2-1/2 cups plain yogurt
2 tablespoons snipped fresh mint leaves
2 tablespoons snipped fresh dill
Ground black pepper, to taste
Pinch Garam Masala, for serving
Pinch paprika, for serving

1. *Place the cucumber in a mesh strainer, sprinkle with salt, and set aside for at least 1 hour. When ready, press the juice out of the cucumbers.*
2. *In a bowl, combine the cucumber, yogurt, mint, dill and pepper. Serve in a bowl with the Garam Masala and paprika on the side.*

Spiced Ginger Sauce

About 1-1/4 cups

3 tablespoons butter or margarine
1 large yellow onion, peeled and chopped
1/4 teaspoon ground coriander
1/4 teaspoon ground ginger
2 tablespoons cornstarch or arrowroot
1-1/2 cups chicken stock or apple juice
1 teaspoon fresh lemon juice
1/2 cup chopped candied ginger
Salt and pepper, to taste

1. *Melt the butter in a saucepan and sauté the onion until translucent. Remove from the heat and stir in the ground coriander and ground ginger.*
2. *In a cup, stir together the cornstarch and 1/2 cup chicken stock until smooth. Stir this and the remaining stock into the onions. Return to the heat, bring to a boil, and cook, stirring constantly, until just thickened. Reduce to a simmer, and cook for about 2 or 3 minutes. Stir in the fresh lemon juice, candied ginger, and salt and pepper to taste and remove from the heat. Sauce can be stored in the refrigerator for up to three weeks. It is a great accompaniment to grilled chicken.*

Far Away Flavors at Home:
Garam Masala, Tamarind, and Thai Spices

You don't need to cross the ocean to experience a hint of the culinary marvels of the East. You can bring home the flavors of exotic countries with a short trip to an ethnic market. Sometimes, chain grocery stores boast such offerings either in the spice aisle or in the ethnic foods aisle.

Traditionally used in the kitchens of northern India, Garam Masala, which means "warm spice blend," is a concoction of spices. There are many variations, some containing as many as 12 spices. Typical ingredients include cumin, nutmeg, coriander, cloves, black pepper, cardamom, and cinnamon. Unlike curry, this enticing blend is usually sprinkled on food after cooking to brighten the overall flavor of the dish.

Tamarind is a word derived from the Arabic *tamarhindi*, which means "Indian date." In Indian cuisine, the sour taste of tamarind is likened to fresh lemon juice. A natural ingredient in Worcestershire sauce, tamarind comes from the seeds or pods of a tall shade tree and has become popular in Indian, Mexican, and Thai cuisine.

Speaking of Thailand, the Asian nation's culinary success relies heavily on its choice of spices. Two of its most popular hot spices come from members of the Capsicum family (see Box on page 159). *Prik kee noo* and the slightly less hot *prik kee far* are both hot chiles commonly used in Thai cuisine. *Pakshee*, which is the same as cilantro, is a popular aromatic plant commonly used. Curly mint is another aromatic used for tea and salads. Popular both in Japan and Thailand, the ginger root is another significant staple. And let's not forget *Takrai*—the lemon grass that is so popular in curry pastes, hot and sour seafood soups, chicken soups, and salads.

Thai Sweet & Hot Chili Sauce

About 3-1/2 cups

1-1/2 cups seedless raisins, plumped in warm water and drained

5 tablespoons cider vinegar

1 tablespoon red pepper flakes

8 medium cloves garlic, peeled

2 fresh red Thai chile peppers, stemmed, seeded, and sliced

1 (8 ounce) can crushed tomatoes

1 (12 ounce) jar plum jam

1 cup plus 1 tablespoon pineapple juice

1/4 cup packed light brown sugar

1. *In a blender or food processor, combine the raisins, vinegar, red pepper flakes, garlic, chiles, and tomatoes. Process on high until smooth.*
2. *In a saucepan, combine the jam, pineapple juice, and sugar. Heat through, and stir in the mixture from the processor. Bring to a boil, reduce to a simmer, and cook, stirring frequently, for about 20 minutes. Serve with poultry, pork, or fish.*

Thai Relish

About 1/3 cup

1 red or green chile pepper, seeded and finely chopped

2 tablespoons chopped onion

1 teaspoon snipped fresh cilantro or parsley

1 teaspoon granulated sugar

3 tablespoons white or red wine vinegar

In a bowl, combine all of the ingredients. Serve with poultry, beef, or pork.

Thai Crab Dipping Sauce

About 2 to 2-1/4 cups

1 (6 ounce) can crabmeat, drained and flaked

1-1/2 cups cream of coconut (not coconut milk)

3 shallots, peeled and minced

1-1/2 teaspoons granulated sugar

1/4 teaspoon tamarind concentrate (see Box, page 134), dissolved in 1 tablespoon hot water

2 green chile peppers, stemmed, seeded, and sliced

1 tablespoon snipped cilantro

In a saucepan, combine the crab and cream of coconut, bring to a boil, reduce to a simmer, and cook, stirring frequently, for about 5 minutes. Add the shallots, sugar, tamarind liquid, and chiles. Return to a boil, reduce to a simmer, and cook, stirring frequently, for about 5 minutes or until the sauce is as thick as mayonnaise. Transfer to a bowl, stir in the cilantro, and serve alongside seafood or chicken.

Pesto Sauce

About 2/3 cup

1-1/2 cups snipped fresh basil leaves
2 medium cloves garlic, peeled and crushed
2 tablespoons pine nuts
1/2 cup extra virgin olive oil
1/2 cup freshly grated Parmesan cheese
Salt and pepper, to taste

In a food processor (a blender is not recommended) combine the basil, garlic, and pine nuts and process on high, drizzling in the oil throughout. When the mixture is creamy, transfer to a bowl and fold in the cheese and salt and pepper to taste. If freezing, omit the cheese and add it just before serving.

Tuscan Herb Butter

About 1 cup

1/2 pound unsalted butter, at room temperature
2 cloves garlic, peeled and crushed
1 teaspoon crushed dried rosemary
1 teaspoon crushed dried lemon thyme
1 teaspoon crushed dried oregano
1 teaspoon crushed dried sage
Salt and pepper, to taste

In a bowl, using an electric mixer, beat together the butter, garlic, rosemary, thyme, oregano, sage, and salt and pepper until smooth. Use a knife, spoon, or your hands to spread the butter evenly over poultry before cooking.

Zucchini Pesto Sauce

About 2/3 cup

1/2 cup extra virgin olive oil
1-1/2 cups snipped fresh basil leaves
1 medium yellow onion, peeled and chopped
1 medium green bell pepper, stemmed, seeded, and chopped
1 medium mild chile pepper, stemmed, seeded, and chopped
1-1/2 cups diced, trimmed zucchini
Salt and pepper, to taste

In a food processor (a blender is not recommended) combine the olive oil, basil, onion, bell pepper, chile pepper, zucchini, and salt and pepper to taste and process on low until just blended.

Parsley Butter

About 5 tablespoons

1/4 cup unsalted butter
1 teaspoon fresh lemon juice
1 tablespoon snipped fresh parsley
Salt, to taste

In a small bowl, using the back of a spoon, cream the butter until smooth. Add the lemon juice, parsley, and salt to taste, blending until smooth. Transfer to a piece of waxed paper and roll into a log. Chill in the refrigerator for about 1 hour before serving atop fish or steamed vegetables.

Country Herb Butter

About 3/4 cup

3/4 cup unsalted butter
1 tablespoon snipped fresh parsley
1 teaspoon fresh lime or lemon juice
1 tablespoon snipped fresh chives
3 to 4 snipped fresh basil leaves

In a blender or food processor, combine the butter, parsley, lime juice, chives, and basil and process on high until smooth. Transfer to a piece of waxed paper and roll into a log. Serve a pat on chops, grilled chicken, steak, hot baked potatoes, grilled corn on the cob, or fresh bread, warm from the oven.

Beer Marinade

About 2 cups

1 (12 ounce) can beer or ale
1/2 cup bottled French dressing
1 medium clove garlic, peeled and crushed
1 teaspoon mustard powder
Salt and pepper, to taste

In a zippered plastic bag, combine the beer, French dressing, garlic, mustard, and salt and pepper to taste. Add meat, poultry, or fish, shake to coat, and refrigerate for at least 2 hours. Marinade will keep, refrigerated, for 2 to 3 months.

Buttermilk Marinade

About 1 quart

1 quart buttermilk
2 tablespoons cider vinegar
1 large white onion, peeled and sliced
2 teaspoons prepared horseradish
1/2 teaspoon crushed dried sage
Salt and pepper, to taste

In a zippered plastic bag, combine the buttermilk, vinegar, onion, horseradish, sage, and salt and pepper to taste. Add chicken or lamb, shake to coat, and refrigerate for at least 2 hours. Marinade will keep, refrigerated, for 1 month.

Celery Ketchup Marinade

About 1-1/2 cups

2/3 cup tomato ketchup
1/2 cup water or apple juice
1/3 cup fresh lemon juice
2 tablespoons Worcestershire sauce
1 teaspoon celery seeds
1 bay leaf
1/2 teaspoon ground black pepper
1/4 teaspoon crushed dried basil
Bottled hot sauce, to taste
Salt, to taste

In a blender or food processor, combine the ketchup, water, lemon juice, Worcestershire sauce, celery seeds, bay leaf, black pepper, basil, hot sauce to taste, and salt to taste. Process on high until smooth. Use as a marinade for beef.

Sesame-Soy Marinade

About 1-3/4 cups

3/4 cup soy sauce
3/4 cup rice wine vinegar
3 tablespoons packed light brown sugar
1 tablespoon sesame oil
2 green onions, chopped
1-1/2 teaspoons dried red pepper flakes, crushed

In a bowl, combine the soy sauce, vinegar, sugar, sesame oil, green onion, and red pepper flakes. Use as a marinade for poultry or fish.

Teriyaki Marinade

About 1/2 cup

2 tablespoons chopped green onions
1-1/2 teaspoons packed light or dark brown sugar
1/4 teaspoon ground ginger
1/4 cup soy sauce
3 tablespoons dry sherry
1 clove garlic, peeled and minced

In a blender or food processor, combine the green onion, sugar, ginger, soy sauce, sherry, and garlic and process on high until smooth. Use as a marinade for pork, beef, or poultry.

Pineapple-Soy Marinade

About 1-1/2 cups

1 (12 ounce) can frozen pineapple juice concentrate, thawed
3 tablespoons soy sauce
1 teaspoon minced fresh ginger root

In a bowl, stir together the pineapple juice, soy sauce, and ginger. Use on the day of preparation as a marinade for fish.

Citrus Soy Marinade

About 3/4 cup

1/4 cup fresh lemon or lime juice
1/4 cup lite soy sauce
1/4 cup canola oil

*In a blender or food processor, combine the lemon juice,
soy sauce, and canola oil and process on low until smooth. Use
on the day of preparation as a marinade for fish.*

Kebab Marinade

About 1-1/2 cups

1 (13 ounce) can onion soup
1/2 cup water
1/4 cup Burgundy or other red wine
2 tablespoons canola oil
1/2 teaspoon garlic powder
2 teaspoons crushed dried basil
Salt and pepper, to taste

*In a blender or food processor combine the onion soup, water,
wine, canola oil, garlic powder, and basil. Process on low until
smooth. Add salt and pepper to taste and use as a marinade for
beef or lamb kebabs.*

Mustard Marinade

About 1/2 cup

2 tablespoons chopped green onions
1/4 cup extra virgin olive oil
2 tablespoons cider vinegar
2 tablespoons prepared mustard
1 large clove garlic, peeled and minced

1. *In a blender or food processor combine the onion, olive oil, vinegar, mustard, and garlic and process on low until smooth. Transfer to a bowl and set aside for about 1 hour.*
2. *When ready, place the items to be marinated in a zippered plastic bag, add the marinade, shake to coat, and refrigerate for at least 2 hours. Use the marinade on the day of preparation.*

Orange-Pepper Marinade

About 1-1/2 cups

1 (12 ounce) can orange juice concentrate, thawed
1-1/2 to 2 teaspoons dried red pepper flakes
Salt, to taste

In a bowl, stir together the orange juice, red pepper flakes, and salt to taste and set aside until ready to use. Use on the day of preparation as a marinade for pork, chicken, or fish.

Red Wine Marinade

About 1-1/4 cups

4 tablespoons extra virgin olive oil
1 large yellow onion, peeled and sliced
1 medium carrot, trimmed, pared, and sliced
1 stalk celery, trimmed and sliced
1 medium clove garlic, peeled and sliced
3 cups red wine
1/2 cup red wine vinegar
10 black peppercorns
Sprig fresh parsley
Sprig fresh thyme
1 bay leaf

1. *Heat the olive oil in a saucepan, add the onion, carrots, celery, and garlic and sauté until the onion is translucent. Add the wine, vinegar, peppercorns, parsley, thyme, and bay leaf. Bring to a boil, reduce to a simmer, cover, and cook for about 15 minutes. Remove from the heat, and let cool completely.*
2. *When ready, place the items to be marinated in a zippered plastic bag, add the marinade, and chill in the refrigerator for at least 24 hours. Use on beef or lambo.*

Poppy Seed Dressing

About 3 cups

1-1/2 cups granulated sugar
2 teaspoons mustard powder
2/3 cup rice wine vinegar
2 teaspoons onion juice
2 cups safflower oil
1 tablespoon poppy seeds
Salt and pepper, to taste

In a blender or food processor, combine the sugar, mustard powder, and vinegar and process on low until smooth. Beat in the onion juice. With the blender running, add the oil in a narrow stream until the dressing has thickened. Add the poppy seeds and salt and pepper and process on low for a few seconds to incorporate.

Mustard-Chive Vinaigrette

1/4 cup extra virgin olive oil
2 tablespoons red wine vinegar
1-1/2 teaspoons snipped fresh chives
1 teaspoon grainy mustard
Salt and pepper, to taste

In a jar with a tightly fitting cover or a small bowl, combine the olive oil, vinegar, chives, mustard, and salt and pepper to taste. Shake the jar vigorously until blended.

Fresh Lime Dressing

About 1-1/2 cups

3 tablespoons fresh lime juice
1/2 cup honey, warm
2 large eggs, beaten
1/2 cup heavy cream, whipped stiff but not dry

In a saucepan, stir together the lime juice, honey, and eggs. Cook, stirring constantly, over a low heat until thickened. Remove from the heat, cool slightly, and fold in the whipped cream. Chill before serving over fresh fruit.

More Main Attractions

Clambake

SIPS AND STARTERS

•

Minted Ginger Tea
Easy Onion Dip

SALADS

•

The Simplest Green Salad

ENTREES

•

Beer-Steamed Clams
Gloucester Fish Chowder
Sherry-Soy Seafood Kebabs with Mango-Ginger Salsa

SIDES

•

Deluxe Coleslaw
Grilled Baked Potatoes

FROM THE BAKERY

•

Spoon Bread
Great Aunt Ida's Easy Yellow Cake with Rich Buttercream Frosting

Chicken Enchilada Casserole

4 to 6 servings

5 cups diced cooked chicken

1/4 cup snipped fresh cilantro

1/2 cup chopped green onion, whites included

1 (4 ounce) can green chiles, drained and chopped

1-1/2 pounds sour cream or plain yogurt

1 tablespoon chili powder

2 tablespoons ground cumin

2 cups picante sauce

6 corn tortillas

3 cups grated cheddar cheese

1. *Position a rack in the center of the oven and preheat to 350° F. Have a rectangular baking dish ready.*
2. *In a large bowl, combine the chicken, cilantro, and green onion.*
3. *In a small bowl, beat together the green chiles, sour cream, chili powder, cumin, and picante sauce.*
4. *In the baking dish, place a layer of tortillas, then a layer of the chicken mixture, and then a layer of the sour cream mixture. Repeat until all ingredients are used up, ending with a layer of cheese. Bake, uncovered, for about 30 minutes, or until the cheese has melted.*

Potato Chip & Chicken Casserole

6 servings

3 cups chopped cooked chicken

2 cups chopped celery

1 cup blanched almond slivers

2 tablespoons minced onion

2 tablespoons fresh lemon juice

1/2 cup sour cream or plain yogurt

1 (10-3/4 ounce) can condensed cream of asparagus soup, undiluted

1 cup shredded cheddar cheese

1 cup crushed barbecue-flavored potato chips

1. *Position a rack in the center of the oven and preheat to 350° F.*
2. *In a medium bowl, combine the chicken, celery, almonds, and onion.*
3. *In another bowl, blend together the lemon juice, sour cream, and asparagus soup.*
4. *Combine the two mixtures, spoon into a casserole or baking dish, and sprinkle the cheese and potato chips over the top. Bake for about 30 minutes or until heated through. Remove from the oven and serve.*

Tuna Noodle Casserole

6 to 8 servings

Oil or shortening, for greasing the pan

1 (6 ounce) package egg noodles, cooked al dente and drained

2 tablespoons butter or margarine, at room temperature

1 (10-1/2 ounce) can cream of mushroom soup

1 cup milk or soy milk

1/2 cup sour cream or plain yogurt

1/2 cup chopped yellow onion

1/2 cup chopped green bell pepper

1 cup chopped celery

1 (6-1/2 ounce) can tuna, or more to taste, drained and flaked

15 Ritz-style round crackers, coarsely broken

1 tablespoon crushed dried parsley

1. *Position a rack in the center of the oven and preheat to 350° F. Lightly grease a 2-quart casserole dish.*

2. *Place the noodles in a large bowl, add the butter, and toss to coat.*

3. *In a saucepan, combine the mushroom soup, milk, sour cream, onion, bell pepper, and celery. Bring to a boil, reduce to a simmer, and stir in the tuna. Heat through and add the noodles.*

4. *Spoon the mixture into the prepared casserole, sprinkle the broken crackers over the top, and bake for about 20 minutes. Garnish with the parsley and serve immediately.*

Clambake: A New England Tradition

Everyone's heard the story about how the Pilgrims shared the first Thanksgiving feast with the Native Americans. Less known is that the Natives first taught European newcomers the art of steaming clams, corn, and other edibles in a hole in the ground. It has since become a beloved New England event called "the Clambake."

To partake of this tasty tradition, first dig a hole in the ground and cover the bottom with large stones. This is the preferred way, but if you're not too hot on the idea of excavating your backyard, a charcoal grill will work just as well. Build your fire on top of the stones and let it burn for a while to heat the stones sufficiently. Meanwhile, prepare your vittles, which can vary but, of course, should include a plentiful amount of fresh clams. Other choice items to consider are lobsters, potatoes, peeled onions, lemons, and butter.

Have enough seaweed on hand to cover the fire pit. (The seaweed releases moisture as it heats, enhancing the effect on the food.) Wire baskets, though not necessary, are helpful in holding everything together. Wrap individual servings of your various ingredients in cheesecloth and tie the corners together before putting them in the baskets. Once the rocks are sauna hot, rake off the coals and cover the rocks with seaweed. Place the food packets on the seaweed, and layer with yet more seaweed. It is recommended that the whole pit be covered with a large tarpaulin. After two hours in the pit—or one hour on the charcoal grill—your feast should be ready and is best served with melted butter, salt and pepper, and ketchup. Be prepared, too, to transform your clam treats into a piping hot chowder with oyster crackers alongside.

Nonna's Famous Lasagna

6 to 8 servings

1 tablespoon butter or margarine

1 pound sweet Italian sausage, casings removed

1 medium clove garlic, peeled and minced

1 tablespoon snipped fresh basil

1 (6 ounce) can tomato paste

1 (16 ounce) can crushed tomatoes

2 extra large eggs

3 cups ricotta or cottage cheese

1/2 cup grated Parmesan cheese

2 tablespoons dried parsley

Salt and pepper, to taste

Oil or shortening, for greasing the pan

1 (6-1/2 ounce) package lasagna pasta,
    cooked al dente and drained

1 pound mozzarella cheese, thinly sliced

1. *Melt the butter in a saucepan or large skillet, and sauté the sausage until no longer pink. Add the garlic, basil, tomato paste, and crushed tomatoes, and simmer, stirring occasionally, for about 5 minutes.*

2. *Meanwhile, in a bowl, beat the eggs until thick, then beat in the ricotta, Parmesan, parsley, and salt and pepper to taste.*

3. *Position a rack in the center of the oven and preheat to 375° F. Lightly grease a 13- x 9-inch baking pan.*

4. *Layer sheets of Lasagna in the bottom of the prepared baking pan, cover with half of the mozzarella, and spoon half the tomato sauce over the top. Repeat until all the ingredients are layered in the pan.*

5. *Bake for about 30 minutes, and remove from the oven. Set aside for about 10 minutes before cutting into serving-size pieces.*

Frito® Pie

4 to 6 servings

Oil or shortening, for greasing the pan

1 tablespoon vegetable oil

1-1/2 pounds lean ground beef

1 large yellow onion, peeled and chopped

1 large green bell pepper, stemmed, seeded, and chopped

1 (8 ounce) package American cheese

1 (15 ounce) can pinto beans

1 (10-1/2 ounce) can tomato soup

1 (6 ounce) jar taco sauce

1 small bag Fritos®, crushed

1. *Position a rack in the center of the oven and preheat to 350° F. Lightly grease a 13- x 9-inch baking pan.*
2. *Heat the oil in a skillet and sauté the beef, mincing with the back of a fork, until no longer pink. Add the onion and bell pepper, and continue cooking until the onion is tender. Remove from the heat and drain off the fat through a sieve.*
3. *Return the mixture to the pan, add half the cheese, and cook, stirring, until melted. Remove from the heat, stir in the beans, tomato soup, taco sauce, and crushed Fritos®. Spread evenly into the prepared baking pan, sprinkle with the remaining cheese, and bake until the cheese topping melts and begins to brown. Remove from the heat and serve immediately.*

Super Sloppy Joes

About 12 servings

2 pounds lean ground beef

1-1/2 cups chopped yellow onion

1/2 cup minced green bell pepper

2 medium cloves garlic, peeled and minced

2/3 cup water

1/2 cup ketchup

2 tablespoons brown mustard

1 teaspoon chili powder

1 teaspoon ground cumin

1 (16 ounce) can tomato sauce

1 (16 ounce) can diced tomatoes

1 (6 ounce) can tomato paste

12 hamburger buns, toasted

1. *In a large saucepan or Dutch oven, combine the beef, onion, bell pepper, and garlic. Sauté, mincing the beef with a fork until it is no longer pink. Remove from the heat, and drain off the fat through a fine sieve.*
2. *Wipe the pot clean, and return the beef mixture to the pot. Add the water, ketchup, mustard, chili powder, cumin, tomato sauce, diced tomatoes, and tomato paste. Bring to a boil, reduce to a simmer, cover lightly, and cook, stirring occasionally, for about 30 minutes. Remove from the heat, and serve over the warm hamburger buns.*

Kidney or black beans can be added if desired.

"Easy As" Chicken Pot Pie

4 to 6 servings

2 (10-3/4 ounce) cans cream of broccoli soup

1 cup milk

1/4 teaspoon crushed dried thyme

1/4 teaspoon ground black pepper

1 cup diced cooked mixed vegetables of choice (such as carrots, potatoes, onion, celery)

2 cups cubed cooked chicken

Salt, to taste

1 (16 ounce) package refrigerated flaky biscuits

1. *Position a rack in the center of the oven and preheat to 400° F. In a casserole dish, stir together the soup, milk, thyme, and pepper. Stir in the vegetables, chicken, and salt to taste. Bake for about 15 minutes, or until bubbly.*

2. *Meanwhile, cut the biscuits into quarters. Arrange the biscuits on top of the cooked chicken mixture. Bake the pot pie for about 15 minutes, or until golden brown.*

Crispy Honey Dip't Chicken

4 to 6 servings

Oil or shortening, for greasing the pan

2/3 cup salad dressing of choice

1 tablespoon honey

2 small chickens (about 2 to 2-1/2 pounds), cut into serving-size pieces

1-3/4 cup crushed corn or wheat flake cereal

1. *Position a rack in the center of the oven and preheat to 375° F. Lightly grease a 13- x 9-inch baking pan.*

2. *In a bowl, blend together the dressing and honey. Dip the chicken into the dressing mixture and roll in the crushed cereal until well coated.*

3. *Arrange the chicken in the prepared baking pan and bake for 35 to 40 minutes or until tender and lightly browned. Remove from the oven and serve.*

Pecan Stuffed Squash

4 to 6 servings

2 small acorn squash, trimmed, halved, and seeded

1-2/3 cup vegetable stock

1/3 cup butter or margarine

2 cups dry herb stuffing mix

1/2 cup chopped pecans

1/3 cup seedless raisins

1/4 cup chopped pimientos

Grated Parmesan cheese, for serving

1. *Position a rack in the center of the oven and preheat to 400° F.*
2. *Arrange the squash halves, cut-side down, in a shallow baking dish. Add 1 cup of the stock, and bake for about 25 minutes.*
3. *Meanwhile, in a saucepan, combine the remaining stock and butter, heating until the butter is melted. Stir in the stuffing mix, pecans, raisins, and pimientos and heat through.*
4. *Using tongs, turn the squash over so it is cut-side up, and spoon the stuffing mixture into the cavities. Continue to bake, basting with the broth from the pan, for about 15 to 20 minutes or until the squash is fork tender. Remove from the oven, top with some grated Parmesan, and serve.*

Eggplant and Tofu Stir-Fry

4 to 6 servings

1 large eggplant, cut into matchsticks

Salt, for sweating the eggplant

3 tablespoons soy sauce

1/4 cup dry sherry

1 tablespoon packed light brown sugar

1 tablespoon cider vinegar

Water

1 tablespoon cornstarch or arrowroot powder

2 tablespoons peanut oil

1 medium yellow onion, peeled and thinly sliced

2 tablespoons minced garlic

1 tablespoon minced fresh ginger root

Salt and pepper, to taste

3 (8 ounce) packages firm tofu

8 green onions, washed and trimmed, with white portion minced and green portion chopped, for garnish

1. *Place the eggplant in a bowl, sprinkle with salt, and set aside.*
2. *In a measuring cup, combine the soy sauce, sherry, sugar, and vinegar and stir until the sugar is dissolved. Add enough water to make 1 cup.*
3. *In a small bowl, blend together the soy mixture and cornstarch, a little at a time, to form a smooth paste. Set aside.*
4. *Heat the oil in a large skillet or wok and sauté the onion, stirring constantly, for about 1 minute. Drain and rinse the eggplant, pat dry using paper towels, and add to the onion, stirring for about 8 minutes, or until the eggplant is fork tender. Add the remaining ingredients and the soy mixture and cook until heated through and the sauce is thickened. Serve over white rice, garnished with chopped green onion.*

A Down-and-Dirty Maryland Crab Boil

From Maryland's shores and southward, crabs are a prized part of the regional cuisine. They also provide the foundation for a great beach party or backyard gathering: a Maryland Crab Boil is an awesome occasion. All you need is a stove, an open fire, or a sturdy-standing grill; and, of course, your food and friends. Assume you'll need between two and four live crabs per person and that your crabs should be as fresh (i.e., still alive) as possible. And bring the extra goodies: shucked ears of corn; red potatoes; white onions; lemons; a few whole bay leaves; and some Old Bay Seasoning.

Combine all the vegetables and seasonings in a large stock pot, and fill it with water so that the crabs can be added, and submerged, later. After the goodies come to a boil, lower the heat (or place the pot over a cooler section of the grill) and simmer until the potatoes are partially cooked, about 10 to 15 minutes. Bring it back to a boil and toss in the crabs. Be careful, though, because they may not be as happy as you are about the arrangement. Cover the pot and simmer for 5 to 7 minutes, or until the crabs turn red. After checking to make sure the potatoes are fully cooked, drain the liquid and serve immediately.

There's nothing fancy about the crab boil: Just lay down a few layers of butcher paper on a table, and provide plenty of napkins and perhaps paper or plastic bibs. For implements of the feast, set out nutcrackers, nut picks, wooden mallets, and other useful tools to crack crab shells and extract the meat. Ditch the formalities—this is a hands-on eating experience that calls for plenty of cold beer, good tunes, and a hefty appetite.

The oldest crab industry in North America—
the blue crab industry of the Chesapeake Bay area—
dates back almost four centuries.

Chili Con Carne

6 to 8 servings

6 tablespoons bacon fat

3 medium yellow onions, peeled and chopped

4 medium cloves garlic, peeled and minced

2 tablespoons chili powder blended with 1 tablespoon flour

1 tablespoon ground cumin

3 pounds lean ground beef

2 (16 ounce) cans crushed tomatoes

1 tablespoon crushed dried oregano

1 tablespoon red wine vinegar

1-1/2 teaspoons packed brown sugar

1 (16 ounce) can red kidney beans

1 (16 ounce) can black olives, chopped (optional)

Salt and pepper, to taste

1. *Melt the bacon fat in a saucepan or Dutch oven and sauté the onions and garlic together until lightly browned. Add the chili powder mixture and cumin and sauté, stirring constantly, to make a roux. Add the beef and cook, mincing with the back of a fork, until no longer pink.*
2. *Stir in 1 can of tomatoes, and simmer slowly for about 10 minutes. Add the oregano, vinegar, and sugar. Cook for about 10 minutes longer, and add the beans. Cover tightly and cook over a low simmer, stirring occasionally, for about 1-1/2 hours.*
3. *Add the remaining tomatoes, and the olives, if desired. Cover lightly and cook for about 20 minutes longer. Remove from the heat, add salt and pepper to taste, and serve.*

Cathedral Chili Con Pollo

4 to 6 servings

2 tablespoons canola oil

1/3 cup finely chopped white onion

1/3 cup finely chopped green or red bell pepper

1 pound ground chicken

1 large clove garlic, minced

1 (16 ounce) can stewed tomatoes

2 (15 ounce) cans kidney beans, drained

1 (16 ounce) can mixed vegetables, liquid reserved

Soft rolls or warm tortillas, for serving

1. *Heat the oil in a medium saucepan or kettle over medium heat. Add the onion and bell pepper and cook, stirring occasionally, until the vegetables are tender. Add the chicken and garlic and continue to cook, stirring and breaking up the chicken, until the chicken is no longer pink. Add the tomatoes and kidney beans, bring to a boil, reduce to a simmer, cover, and cook for 30 minutes.*
2. *Add the mixed vegetables and cook until heated through. Remove from the heat and serve with rolls or tortillas on the side.*

Pick a Pepper: All About the Capsicum

There are hundreds of varieties of pepper on the planet, ranging in length from 1/2 inch to 12 inches. All are members of the genus Capsicum, which originates from the Greek word *kapto*, meaning, "to bite." Here's some special ones you should meet:

- CAYENNE PEPPER *is a small chile with a good degree of heat. It's usually used in a dried, powdered form to be sprinkled on food.*

- JALAPEÑO *is one of the more common chiles in North American foods. It's typically served raw or pickled to spice up nachos and other semi-spicy delectables.*

- CHIPOTLE, *pronounced "chee-pot-lay," is a smoked jalapeño common in Mexican fare and salsas.*

- HABAÑERO *arguably has the strongest bite of all peppers, with a Scotch bonnet following in close second. The tiny, round-shaped red, green, or yellow fruit has an intense fire that can irritate bare skin on contact.*

- POBLANO *is a larger, narrow chile that has a sweet, zippy flavor somewhat similar to a bell pepper, but with a bit of heat, and is great for stuffing.*

Vegetarian Chili

6 to 8 servings

1-1/4 cups cooked red kidney beans
1 medium yellow onion, peeled and minced, divided
2 medium cloves garlic, peeled and minced
1-1/4 cups minced carrots
1-1/4 cups minced green beans
1/2 cup green or red bell pepper, minced, stemmed, and seeded
1/4 cup water
1/2 teaspoon chili powder
1/2 teaspoon cumin
Jalapeño pepper, stemmed, seeded, and minced
1 (15 ounce) can stewed tomatoes
1 (6 ounce) can tomato paste
Shredded cheddar or Monterey Jack cheese, for serving

1. *Position a rack in the center of the oven and preheat to 350° F.*
2. *In a bowl, combine the kidney beans, onion, garlic, carrots, green beans, bell pepper, water, chili powder, cumin, jalapeño, tomatoes, and tomato paste. Spoon into a casserole dish, and bake for about 20 minutes, or until the green beans are tender. Remove from the oven and serve topped with shredded cheese, if desired.*

Eggplant Tofu Curry

About 4 to 6 servings

4 small eggplants

1/2 cup canola oil

4 small yellow onions, peeled and chopped

3 tablespoons minced garlic

1/4 teaspoon ground black pepper

1/4 teaspoon red pepper flakes

1/2 teaspoon ground turmeric

2 teaspoons ground coriander

1 (16 ounce) can chopped tomatoes

2 (14 ounce) packages extra firm tofu, drained and cubed

2 teaspoons Garam Masala (see page 134)

1/2 cup snipped fresh cilantro

1. *Position a rack in the center of the oven and preheat to 400° F.*
2. *Using the tines of a fork, punch several holes around each eggplant, and bake for about 40 to 45 minutes, or until fork tender. Remove from the oven, cool, peel and roughly chop.*
3. *Heat the oil in a saucepan or skillet, and sauté the onion and garlic together until the onion is translucent. Add the black pepper, red pepper flakes, turmeric, and coriander. Heat through, and add the tomatoes and eggplant. Cook for about 3 minutes, and add the tofu and Garam Masala. Remove from the heat, garnish with cilantro, and serve.*

Bivalves & Brew: The Delicious Art of Beer-Steamed Clams

Some say with steadfast determination, "nothing beats a cold can of beer on a hot day." Others protest, "Nay! Beer is good, but better for steaming clams than guzzling cans!" Of the latter sentiment's verity, you can explore for yourself. To make great beer-steamed clams, proceed gently, with beer on hand, to your culinary laboratory.

- *For four servings, wash two dozen cherrystone-size clams thoroughly under cold running water. Place the clams in the bottom of a clam steamer or large pot. Add enough beer—about 12 ounces—to cover between one and two inches of the bottom. Cover and bring beer to a boil and steam until the clams at the top open just barely (about 3 to 5 minutes). Beware not to overcook—clams can easily turn tough and rubbery. Prepare a Garlic Butter Dip by sautéing a clove of chopped garlic and a generous pinch of fresh parsley in a stick of melted salted butter.*

Dip your clams and decide for yourself: cold beer, or beer-steamed clams? Or better yet, enjoy both. Can't we all just get along?

Latin Black Bean Soup

About 6 servings

1 cup dried black beans, sorted, rinsed,
  and soaked in water overnight
8 cups water
1 onion, peeled and chopped
1 green bell pepper, stemmed, seeded, and chopped
2 cloves garlic, peeled and crushed
1 teaspoon dried oregano
1 teaspoon ground cumin
1 (6 ounce) can tomato paste
3 tablespoons red wine vinegar
1 tablespoon Tamari soy sauce
2 cups cooked brown rice
1/4 cup green chiles, stemmed, seeded, and chopped
1/4 teaspoon bottled hot sauce
2 tablespoons snipped fresh cilantro
Chopped red bell peppers, for garnish
Sour cream, for garnish

1. *Place the beans and water in a large soup pot, bring to a boil, and cook for 2 minutes. Remove from the heat, cover, and let rest for about 45 minutes. Return to the heat, and add the onion, bell pepper, garlic, oregano, and cumin. Cover and let cook over low heat for 1-1/2 hours.*
2. *Add the tomato paste, vinegar, and soy sauce and cook for an additional 30 minutes. Add the rice, chiles, hot sauce, and cilantro, and cook for 10 more minutes. Serve hot.*

This soup is very spicy—
to tame it a bit
feel free to omit the
chiles or hot sauce.

Gloucester Fish Chowder

6 to 8 servings

1/3 cup butter or margarine

1 cup diced new potatoes

1/2 cup chopped yellow onion

1/2 cup sliced fresh mushrooms

1/4 cup diced red bell pepper

1 pound skinless white fish filets, such as cod or haddock, cut into
   3/4-inch cubes

1 (10-3/4 ounce) can condensed cream of celery soup

1 (10-3/4 ounce) can condensed cream of potato soup

2 cups milk

1/4 cup dry white wine

2 (10 ounce) packages frozen whole kernel corn, thawed

2 tablespoons diced pimiento

Salt and pepper, to taste

1. *On the stove over medium heat, melt the butter in a soup kettle and sauté the potatoes, onion, mushrooms, and red pepper for about 10 minutes. Add the fish, and cook, stirring, for about 10 minutes.*
2. *In a bowl, blend together the celery soup, potato soup, milk, and white wine. Stir into the soup kettle.*
3. *Stir in the corn, bring to a boil, reduce to a simmer, and add the pimiento and salt and pepper to taste.*
4. *Transfer to the coolest part of the grill to keep warm, if serving as part of a barbecue.*

Harvest Corn Chowder

10 to 12 servings

1 tablespoon butter or margarine

1 medium onion, peeled and chopped

2 (14-1/2 ounce) cans creamed corn

4 cups whole kernel corn

4 cups diced, peeled potatoes

1 (10-3/4 ounce) can condensed cream of mushroom soup, undiluted

1 (6 ounce) can sliced mushrooms, drained

3 cups milk

1/2 medium green bell pepper, stemmed, seeded, and chopped

1/2 medium red bell pepper, stemmed, seeded, and chopped

Salt and pepper, to taste

1/2 pound bacon, cooked and crumbled, for garnish

1. *In a saucepan, melt the butter, add the onion, and sauté until tender. Add the creamed corn, kernel corn, potatoes, mushroom soup, and sliced mushrooms. Stir in the milk, green and red peppers, and salt and pepper to taste.*
2. *Let simmer for about 30 minutes or until the vegetables are tender. Remove from the heat, garnish with the crumbled bacon, and serve.*

Andouille-Shrimp Gumbo

6 to 8 servings

1/4 cup olive oil

1-1/2 pounds andouille sausage, sliced into 1/2-inch-thick pieces

1 cup flour

3 cups chopped yellow onion

3 cloves garlic, minced

2 cups chopped celery

2 green bell peppers, cored, seeded, and chopped

8-1/2 cups chicken stock

1 pound frozen uncooked peeled deveined shrimp, thawed

1 teaspoon cayenne pepper

1 teaspoon filé powder

1 cup cream sherry

Salt and pepper, to taste

1 cup cooked rice

2 cups chopped green onion

1. *Heat the oil in a soup kettle or large pot over medium-high heat. Add the sausage and cook until it is browned on all sides.*
2. *Using a slotted spoon, remove and sausage from the kettle and set aside. Add the flour to the oil in the kettle and cook, stirring constantly, until the mixture thickens and browns. Add the onion, garlic, celery, and green bell pepper, stirring constantly, until the onion is tender. Return the sausage to the pan and gradually stir in the chicken stock until smooth. Reduce to a simmer, cover, and cook for about 1 hour.*
3. *Add the shrimp, cayenne pepper, filé powder, and sherry, stirring to incorporate. Cook for about 5 minutes, or until shrimp are pink and firm. Add salt and pepper to taste and remove from heat. Stir in the rice and green onion and serve.*

Born on the Bayou: A Cajun-Style Clambake

For a bayou-style clambake, refer to the box on the New England Clambake (see page 151) and spin it into a Cajun affair. Use lots of cayenne pepper and Tabasco sauce to season those fat and juicy Gulf shrimp, crawdads, crabs, oysters, or scallops. Toss some okra and perhaps some spicy alligator sausage into the mix.

Consider serving up Andouille-Shrimp Gumbo (see this page), which is a particularly popular homemade dish during the wintertime. Serve it over rice, and listen for the instinctive "mm'mm"s coming from your guests' lips. Better yet, set these sounds of reveling satisfaction to an uppity beat with some good, appropriate music: Buckwheat Zydeco, Beau Jocque, the Zydeco All-Stars, the Zydeco Hi-Rollers—to name just a few.

Italian Lamb Stew

4 to 6 servings

Oil or shortening, for greasing the pot

3/4 pound boneless leg of lamb, trimmed and cubed

1/2 cup all-purpose flour

4 cups water

1 tablespoon Italian seasoning

Salt and pepper, to taste

4 bay leaves

1 large clove garlic, peeled and minced

3 medium red potatoes, peeled and wedged

1 cup sliced carrots

1 cup chopped white onion

1. *Position a rack in the center of the oven and preheat to 350° F. Lightly grease a large Dutch oven.*

2. *In a plastic bag, combine the lamb cubes and flour and shake to coat. Shake any excess flour back into the bag and place the coated lamb on a plate. Reserve the remaining flour.*

3. *Place the Dutch oven over medium heat, add the lamb, and cook slowly, stirring frequently, until lightly browned on all sides. Remove the pot from the heat, and set aside.*

4. *Transfer the remaining flour from the plastic bag to a bowl, and whisk in 1 cup of the water until smooth. Pour the mixture over the lamb and add the remaining water, Italian seasoning, salt and pepper, bay leaves, garlic, potatoes, carrots, and onion. Return to the heat, bring to a boil, cover, and transfer to the oven.*

5. *Bake for about 1 hour, or until the lamb is very tender. Remove from the oven, discard the bay leaves, and serve over cooked rice, if desired.*

Brown Ale Beef Stew

4 to 6 servings

2 tablespoons unsalted butter

4 shallots, peeled and diced

2 pounds boneless chuck roast, trimmed and cubed

2 tablespoons all-purpose flour

1/4 teaspoon ground coriander

2 sprigs fresh thyme

2 tablespoons brown mustard

3-1/2 cups brown ale

1 (8 ounce) package baby carrots, roughly chopped

1. *Melt the butter in a Dutch oven, add the shallots, and sauté until tender. Add the beef and cook, stirring frequently, until no longer pink.*
2. *Sprinkle on the flour and cook, stirring until incorporated. Add the coriander, thyme, and mustard. Stir in the ale, bring to a boil, and reduce to a simmer.*
3. *Add the carrots, cover tightly and cook gently, stirring occasionally, for about 1-1/2 hours. Remove from the heat and serve immediately over cooked potatoes or rice.*

Let Them Bring the Party to You: Potlucks and More

What better way to get guests involved at your next shindig than by throwing a potluck, salsa contest, chili cookoff, or wine-tasting fete? For a potluck, list categories of foods on your invite: international; salads; casseroles; desserts. For a salsa contest, separate entries into hot, mild, and medium, and perhaps those that contain non-conventional items—the mango-green chile salsa may be a pleasant surprise. For a chili cookoff, designate random judges making sure you are among them—and feast away. For wine sampling, have your friends bring their favorite vintage, along with cheeses to complement them. Such ideas can save you energy preparing for a large gathering, while furnishing a great way for you and your guests to experience a variety of new palate-pleasers.

Sizzling Sides

Tailgate Party

SIPS AND STARTERS

•

Wine Cooler
Mulled Cider
Snack Scramble
Tortilla Bites

SALADS

•

Santa Fe Salad

ENTREES

•

Barbecued Beef Short Ribs
Coney Island Hot Dogs
Vegetarian Chili

SIDES

•

Red & Green Rice
Fusilli with Spinach, Tomato, & Feta Cheese

FROM THE BAKERY

•

Herbed Tomato Bread
Butterscotch Cheesecake Bars

Grilled Carrots

6 to 8 servings

2 tablespoons safflower oil
1 tablespoon honey soy sauce, (see page 28)
Pinch ginger powder
1 (16 ounce) package frozen baby carrots

1. *In a small bowl, stir together the oil, soy sauce and ginger powder until smooth.*
2. *Place the carrots in a saucepan and parboil for about 5 minutes. Immediately remove from the heat, drain, and shock in cold water.*
3. *Divide carrots into groups of 4 or 5, and lay on a flat surface side by side. Carefully work a bamboo skewer through the center of each bundle, brush with the ginger mixture, and grill on high, turning and basting frequently, until lightly browned.*

Asparagus Two Ways with Garlic Honey Soy Sauce

4 to 6 servings

2 tablespoons peanut oil
1 tablespoon honey soy sauce (see page 28)
1 tablespoon minced garlic
1 to 1-1/2 pounds asparagus, rinsed and trimmed, white ends discarded
Chopped red onion, for serving

SAUTÉED VARIATION

1. *Heat the oil in a skillet over medium heat, and add the soy sauce and garlic. Sauté the garlic until tender.*
2. *Lay half the asparagus in the skillet, and sauté, turning, until lightly browned on all sides. Transfer to a warming dish and cook the remaining asparagus. Sprinkle with the chopped onion and serve immediately.*

GRILLED VARIATION

1. *In a saucepan, combine the oil, soy sauce, and garlic. Bring to a boil, and immediately remove from the heat.*
2. *Separate the asparagus into groups of four or five, and lay out on a flat surface. Join each group together with two thin bamboo skewers threaded through the top and bottom of each asparagus. Brush with the garlic mixture. Place the skewered asparagus on a hot barbecue and grill, turning frequently and brushing with the garlic mixture, until lightly colored. Remove from the heat, sprinkle with the chopped onion, and serve immediately.*

Grilled Corn on the Cob

4 servings

4 ears of corn, shucked

6 tablespoons flavored butter of choice (see pages 137 to 138,
   or Box below), at room temperature

Salt and pepper, to taste

*Preheat the grill to high. When the grill is hot, brush each ear of
corn with a bit of the butter, and place on the grill. Cook the corn,
occasionally turning and brushing with the butter, for about 8 to
12 minutes, or until the ears are slightly charred. Remove the
corn from the grill, season to taste with salt and pepper, and
serve immediately.*

Butter Beautiful: Making Your Own Flavored Butter

With ingredients such as herbs, nuts, citrus juice, garlic, honey, ginger, and vegetables, flavors can be added to butter to make just the right topping for grilled meats, fish, and poultry. For savory sauces on fish or meat, think basil-garlic butter, lemon-dill butter, and garlic-pepper butter. For sweet spreadables, think honey butter sprinkled with cinnamon.

Whatever the ingredients, the butter must first be creamed with a wooden spoon or, for larger amounts, an electric mixer. Toss in your desired ingredients and mix together thoroughly—they should be evenly distributed throughout. (Boiled or steamed veggies can be chopped and added, but make sure they have cooled before adding them to the butter.) When you're finished mixing, roll the butter into logs on waxed or parchment paper and chill before serving.

Savory Grilled Tomatoes

12 servings

3 tablespoons extra virgin olive oil, plus extra for brushing the rack

2 tablespoons minced garlic

6 medium ripe tomatoes, halved horizontally

Garlic salt, to taste

1 tablespoon snipped fresh lemon thyme

1 tablespoon snipped fresh oregano

Parmesan or Pecorino Romano cheese, optional

1. *On a grill, position a rack 6 inches from the heat source, brush lightly with oil, and preheat to high.*
2. *Heat the remaining 3 tablespoons of the oil in a skillet, and sauté the garlic until just golden. Transfer to a small bowl, and set aside.*
3. *Sprinkle the halved tomatoes with the garlic salt to taste.*
4. *Place the tomatoes on the grill rack, cut-side down, and cook for about 3 minutes. Using tongs, turn the tomatoes 90 degrees, and continue to cook for about 2 to 3 minutes. Turn the tomatoes cut-side up, and spoon the sautéed garlic over the top of each. Sprinkle with the thyme, oregano, and cheese, and once cheese melts remove from the grill and serve.*

Honey Balsamic Grilled Onions

4 to 6 servings

3 large yellow onions, peeled and cut into 1/2-inch thick slices

Extra virgin olive oil, for basting

1/2 teaspoon balsamic vinegar

3 tablespoons honey, warm

1-1/2 tablespoons soy sauce

1. *On a grill, position a rack about 4 to 6 inches from the heat source and preheat to high.*
2. *Liberally brush the onions with olive oil, place on the rack and grill, turning and basting frequently, for about 20 minutes or until very tender.*
3. *In a bowl, whisk together the vinegar, honey, and soy sauce. Just before the onions are removed from the barbecue, brush liberally with the honey mixture, heat through, and serve immediately.*

Garden Goodies on the Grill

Summer means baseball, cutting the lawn, and having friends and family over for a good old barbecue or cookout. Each season, an abundance of hot dogs, burgers, steak, grilled chicken, and fish is consumed. What people sometimes forget when firing up the grill is that this summer symbol of good times, lazy days, and delicious meat, can also jazz up items from the harvest as well. Grilling vegetables—corn, peppers, zucchini, squash, onions, even tomatoes—concentrates their natural flavors while allowing their outsides to gain a seared, pleasantly smoky flavor.

Prepare the grill by pre-heating it at medium to high and brushing the grates with olive oil or marinade. Veggies can marinate for a half hour at room temperature, or two hours in the fridge. They should be cut into equal sizes prior to grilling, and slower-cooking vegetables like potatoes should be blanched first. On the grill, brush your veggies with the marinade and flip them often. The finished product should be lightly browned, not charred, with visible grill marks. And it should taste great.

Grill-Roasted Onions

8 servings

4 medium yellow or white onions, unpeeled
1 tablespoon extra virgin olive oil
Salt and pepper, to taste
1/2 cup butter or margarine

1. *Using a sharp knife, halve the unpeeled onions. Brush liberally with the oil, and arrange on an 18- x 18-inch square of aluminum foil. Sprinkle with salt and pepper to taste, and drop 1 tablespoon of butter into the center of each onion half.*
2. *Pull up the sides and ends of the foil, and seal tightly.*
3. *Preheat the grill to high.*
4. *Place the aluminum pouch on the grill, turning occasionally, for about 15 to 20 minutes, or until onions are very tender.*
5. *Remove from the heat, and serve immediately with garlic butter (see Box on page 171) on the side.*

Barbecued Garlic

6 to 8 servings

2 large heads garlic
Extra virgin olive oil, for basting

1. *Arrange a piece of aluminum foil on the grill rack and preheat to high.*
2. *Remove the thin outer skins of the garlic, keeping the head intact. Brush the head with, or dip in, the oil.*
3. *Place the garlic on the foil, cover lightly with a pan or pot lid, and cook, basting frequently with oil, for about 30 minutes, or until very tender.*
4. *Remove from the heat, and serve the individual head as is, or squeeze out the cloves and use as a spread on warm, crusty bread.*

Raising the Tailgate Stakes: Game Pools

Increase the stakes at the next tailgate festivities by starting up some game pools. These can be based on odds, players' statistics, final score spreads—you name it. Have your fellow tailgaters ante up something other than cash—and award winners with prizes. If each player tosses an appetizer into the pot, for example, the winner may have a veritable feast on his hands. Of course, it's all in the name of fun, and it's safe to assume that the winner will at least share a nacho or two with the losers.

Dad's Baked Beans

6 to 8 servings

6 slices bacon, diced

1/2 cup thinly sliced onion

1/2 cup diced celery

1 tablespoon minced garlic

1 cup tomato ketchup

1 (15 ounce) can red kidney beans, drained, 1/2 cup liquid reserved

1/2 teaspoon bottled hot sauce

1 (15 ounce) can baby lima beans, drained

1. *In a saucepan, sauté the bacon, stirring frequently, until crisp. Drain all but 1 tablespoon of the drippings from the pan, and add the onion, celery, and garlic. Continue to cook, stirring, until the onion is golden.*
2. *Add the ketchup, kidney beans with liquid, hot sauce, and lima beans and cover the saucepan. Place on the coolest part of the barbecue, and cook, stirring occasionally, for about 20 minutes. Remove from heat and serve—the beans will stay warm for a while.*

Succotash

4 to 6 servings

1 tablespoon extra virgin olive oil

1 medium red onion, peeled and chopped

3 cups frozen whole kernel corn, thawed

2 (10 ounce) packages frozen baby lima beans

Salt and pepper, to taste

1/2 cup snipped fresh parsley

Heat the oil in a saucepan, add the onion, and sauté until translucent. Add the corn, adjust the heat to a low simmer, cover tightly, and cook, stirring occasionally, for about 10 to 15 minutes, or until the corn is heated through. Add the lima beans, salt and pepper to taste, and parsley, and cook, stirring, for about 3 to 4 minutes. Remove from the heat and serve immediately.

Beijing Broccoli

4 to 6 servings

3 cups fresh broccoli florets

1-1/2 cups sliced celery

1 tablespoon peanut oil

1/4 cup chopped green onion

2 tablespoons chopped pimiento

1 (10-3/4 ounce) can chicken gravy

1 tablespoon soy sauce

Salt and pepper, to taste

Chopped cashews, for garnish

1. *Place the broccoli and celery in a saucepan, add water to cover and salt to taste. Bring to a boil, cover, and simmer for about 7 to 10 minutes, or until fork tender. Remove from the heat and drain.*
2. *In a saucepan, heat the oil over medium heat and sauté the green onion and pimiento until just heated through. Add the broccoli, celery, gravy, and soy sauce. Bring to a slow boil and remove from heat.*
3. *Add salt and pepper to taste, and spoon into a serving bowl. Sprinkle with the cashews and serve.*

Taipei Vegetable Stir-fry

6 to 8 servings

3 tablespoons peanut oil

2 medium carrots, trimmed, pared, and cut into 2-inch long pieces

1 medium yellow onion, peeled and thinly sliced

2 cups snow peas, rinsed and patted dry

1/2 teaspoon sugar

1 (15 ounce) can whole baby corn, liquid drained

Salt or soy sauce, to taste

Sesame seeds, for garnish

Red chile pepper, sliced, for garnish

Heat the oil in a large skillet or wok over high heat. Add the carrots, onion, and snowpeas and stir frequently for about 3 minutes. Add the sugar and corn, cover, and cook for about 5 minutes longer, or until the carrots are tender but still crisp. Season with salt or soy sauce, toss with sesame seeds and sliced chile peppers, and serve.

Summer Vegetable Feast

6 to 8 servings

4 slices bacon

12 shallots, peeled and sliced

1/4 cup diced green bell pepper

1 cup hot water

1 cup unsweetened apple juice, warm

1 pound fresh green beans, stemmed, trimmed, and
   sliced crosswise

6 medium ears of corn, shucked, and cut into thirds

2 tablespoons sugar

5 small zucchini, trimmed and sliced into thick rounds

2 stalks celery, chopped

1 large tomato, stemmed, and cut into wedges

Salt and pepper, to taste

1. *In a large saucepan or Dutch oven, cook the bacon until crisp. Transfer to a paper towel to drain.*
2. *In the bacon drippings sauté the shallots and green pepper until the shallots are golden. Add the water, juice, green beans, corn, and sugar. Bring to a boil, reduce to a simmer, cover lightly, and cook for about 10 minutes.*
3. *Add the zucchini and celery, cover and cook for an additional 10 minutes, or until all the vegetables are tender.*
4. *Using a slotted spoon, transfer the vegetables to a platter, and crumble the bacon over the top. Arrange the tomatoes around the edge of the platter, add salt and pepper to taste, and serve immediately.*

Cabbage & Apples

6 to 8 servings

1-1/2 cups butter or margarine

1/3 cup fresh lemon juice

1/4 cup packed light brown sugar

1/4 cup unsweetened apple juice

1/2 teaspoon caraway seeds

4 cups shredded red cabbage

3 medium Macintosh apples, cored, peeled, and chopped

Melt the butter in a saucepan and add the lemon juice, sugar, apple juice, and caraway seeds. Bring to a boil, add the cabbage and apples, and return to a boil. Reduce to a simmer and cover lightly, stirring occasionally, for about 20 minutes.

French Fried Onion Rings

6 to 8 servings

2 to 3 inches of oil, for deep frying
3/4 cup all-purpose flour
1/2 cup unsweetened apple juice
1/2 cup milk or soy milk
6 tablespoons white cornmeal
1 tablespoon extra virgin olive oil
1/2 teaspoon sugar
1/4 teaspoon red pepper flakes
Salt and pepper, to taste
2 large yellow or white onions, peeled, sliced widthwise,
   and separated into rings

1. *Preheat the oil in a skillet, saucepan, or deep fryer.*
2. *In a blender combine the flour, juice, milk, cornmeal, olive oil, sugar, red pepper flakes, and salt and pepper to taste. Process on high until smooth and transfer the batter to a bowl.*
3. *When the oil is heated to around 350 to 375° F, dip the onion rings in the batter, a few at a time, allowing the excess batter to drip back into the bowl. Transfer the dipped rings to the heated oil and fry, turning with a long-handled fork or tongs, for about 2 to 3 minutes, or until golden brown. Transfer to a wire rack covered with paper towels to drain, and continue with the remaining rings. Serve immediately.*

Sauteéd Zucchini with Tomatoes & Herbs

6 to 8 servings

1/4 cup butter or margarine
4 cups sliced fresh zucchini
1/4 cup chopped yellow onion
1-1/2 cups halved cherry tomatoes
3 tablespoons tomato juice
Pinch crushed dried oregano
Pinch crushed dried thyme
Pinch crushed dried basil
Salt and pepper, to taste

1. *Melt the butter in a skillet over medium heat, and add the zucchini and onion and cook, stirring, until the zucchini is tender but still crisp.*
2. *Add the tomatoes, tomato juice, oregano, thyme, and basil and heat through. Add salt and pepper to taste and serve.*

Touchdown! Winning Tailgate Party Tips

What better way to protest the end of summer than to keep its party spirit alive when football season gets underway? At the heart of the tailgate party is an admirable trait—a love of the outdoors that transcends the inconvenience of inclement weather. After all, should weather ever preclude a good time? To have a great tailgate party, remember these few tips:

- *Bring food that can be cooked and brought to the event, or bring a proper grill to cook food on location. Bring bottle openers and corkscrews.*

- *Bring a heavy cloth on which to spread the meal as a buffet-style setup on the tailgate of a pickup truck, or bring a folding table.*

- *Bring some folding chairs, and don't forget plenty of blankets and sweaters and a thermos of hot cocoa or soup to warm up cold carousers.*

- *Bring disposable plates and cups, and a sufficient amount of paper towels. Clean up after yourself so as not to tarnish the name of the tailgating tradition.*

With a little bit of planning, the best of times are still to be had. Just because summer's ending, it doesn't mean the party's over.

Creamy Spinach Casserole

5 to 6 servings

1 (8 ounce) package cream cheese, at room temperature
1/4 cup milk or soy milk
2 (10 ounce) packages frozen chopped spinach, cooked
    and drained
1/3 cup freshly grated Parmesan cheese (see Note)
Salt and pepper, to taste

1. *In a small bowl, stir together the cream cheese and milk until smooth.*
2. *Arrange the spinach in a 1-quart casserole or other ovenproof baking dish. Spoon the cream cheese mixture over the top, sprinkle with the Parmesan cheese, add salt and pepper to taste, cover with aluminum foil, and cook on outer edge of the barbecue rack for about 20 minutes.*
3. *Remove from the heat, but do not remove the foil until just before ready to serve.*

Although pre-grated Parmesan cheese can be used, freshly grated Parmesan cheese has a milder flavor, and is better suited to this casserole.

Carrot Nut Pudding

6 to 8 servings

1 pound carrots, trimmed, pared, and grated
1-1/2 cups milk or enriched rice milk
1/2 cup heavy cream
1 tablespoon all-purpose flour
1 cup ground blanched almonds
1/2 cup packed light brown sugar
1/4 cup safflower oil
1/4 cup raisins
1/2 teaspoon turmeric powder
1/4 teaspoon ground nutmeg or mace
Sliced almonds, for garnish

1. *In a saucepan over medium heat combine the carrots and milk.*
2. *In a cup combine the cream and flour and stir until smooth. Pour over the carrots. Bring to a slow boil and cook, uncovered and stirring frequently, until most of the liquid has evaporated. Reduce to a slow simmer, and stir in the almonds, sugar, oil, raisins, turmeric, and nutmeg and cook, stirring frequently, for 7 to 10 minutes.*
3. *Remove from the heat, transfer to a serving dish, garnish with sliced almonds, and serve.*

Savory Stuffed Eggplants

6 to 12 servings

3 small to medium eggplants, stemmed and halved lengthwise

Salt, to taste

1 tablespoon extra virgin olive oil

1 small yellow onion, peeled and chopped

1/4 cup diced red bell pepper

2 tablespoons minced celery

1 tablespoon minced garlic

1/2 pound lean ground pork

1/2 pound lean ground beef

1 (16 ounce) can crushed tomatoes

1 teaspoon bottled hot sauce

1/2 teaspoon crushed dried French thyme

1/2 teaspoon crushed dried oregano

1/2 cup breadcrumbs

3/4 cup freshly grated Pecorino cheese

1. *Place the eggplant halves in a saucepan, just cover with water, add salt to taste, and bring to a boil. Cook, uncovered, for 15 to 20 minutes. Remove from the heat, drain, and place cut side down on a wire rack to cool.*

2. *When the eggplant is cool to the touch, carefully scoop out the pulp without puncturing the outer skin. Dice the pulp into bite-size pieces.*

3. *Preheat the barbecue to high.*

4. *Heat the oil in a skillet over medium heat, add the onion, and sauté until translucent. Add the bell pepper, celery, and garlic and cook until tender. Add the pork and beef, and cook, breaking into pieces, until no longer pink. Drain the fat from the pan, and stir in the diced eggplant, tomatoes, hot sauce, thyme, and oregano, and simmer until heated through.*

5. *Remove from the heat and stir in the breadcrumbs and 1/2 cup of the cheese. Spoon the mixture into the eggplant shells, pressing it in gently, and sprinkle with the remaining cheese. Wrap with aluminum foil, and place on barbecue for about 15 minutes. Remove from the heat, unwrap, and serve immediately.*

Grilled Baked Potatoes

6 servings

6 large Idaho potatoes
Extra virgin olive oil, for brushing potatoes

1. *Position the barbecue rack 6 inches from the heat source and preheat to high.*
2. *Thoroughly wash and dry the potatoes, brush liberally with the olive oil, place on the grill, and bake, turning, for about 1 hour or until fork tender.*

This method may make the skin look dried out—to avoid this, brush occasionally with oil while baking or wrap the potatoes in small squares of aluminum foil, place 4 inches from the heat source, and bake, turning, for about 40 minutes.

Barbecue Roasted Sweet Potatoes

6 servings

Vegetable oil, for the rack
6 large sweet potatoes or yams
Butter and brown sugar, for serving

1. *Position the grill rack 4 inches from the heat source, brush with vegetable oil, and preheat to high.*
2. *Use tongs to carefully lay the potatoes on the hot embers. Roast the potatoes, turning occasionally with the tongs, until the skins are black and the potatoes are fork tender, about 40 minutes to 1 hour.*
3. *Remove from the barbecue, and serve immediately with butter and brown sugar on the side.*

Fancy Macaroni & Cheese

8 to 10 servings

1 pound elbow macaroni, cooked al dente and drained

3 tablespoons butter or margarine

1 medium yellow onion, peeled and diced

2 tablespoons all-purpose flour

1/4 teaspoon ground black pepper

1/4 teaspoon cayenne pepper

1/4 teaspoon ground nutmeg or mace

4 cups milk or soy milk

1/2 cup grated Parmesan cheese

1 (4 ounce) package bleu cheese, crumbled

1. *Position a rack in the center of the oven and preheat to 350° F.*
2. *Melt the butter in a large saucepan, and sauté the onion until translucent. Sprinkle on the flour, and stir until the mixture thickens. Stir in the black pepper, cayenne pepper, and nutmeg, and cook briefly, stirring frequently. Pouring in a narrow stream, add the milk, and cook, stirring constantly, until it comes to a slow boil, or until thickened. Stir in 1/4 cup of the Parmesan cheese and all of the bleu cheese, heat through until melted and incorporated, and remove from the heat.*
3. *Stir the cheese mixture into the drained pasta, and transfer to a 3-quart casserole dish.*
4. *Sprinkle the remaining Parmesan cheese over the casserole. Place in the oven and bake for about 20 minutes, or until very hot and bubbly. Remove from the heat and serve immediately.*

Fusilli with Spinach, Tomato, & Feta Cheese

4 to 6 servings

1 pound fusilli or other short pasta

4 tablespoons extra virgin olive oil

1 medium yellow onion, chopped

2 cloves garlic, crushed

1 (16 ounce) package frozen chopped spinach, thawed and drained

6 cups ripe cherry tomatoes

1 cup crumbled feta cheese, or to taste

1. *Bring a large pot of salted water to a boil. Add the pasta and cook according to package directions, or until al dente.*
2. *Meanwhile, heat the olive oil over medium heat and sauté the onion and garlic until golden. Add the spinach and heat through. Remove from the heat, place in a large bowl and stir in the tomatoes.*
3. *Add the drained pasta and toss (you may need to add a touch more olive oil). Stir in the feta cheese while the pasta is still hot, and serve immediately or at room temperature.*

Shells with Broccoli & Fresh Tarragon

4 to 6 servings

1 pound small pasta shells
1 (10 ounce) package frozen chopped broccoli
2 tablespoons extra virgin olive oil
2 tablespoons minced yellow onion
1 tablespoon snipped fresh tarragon
1 small clove garlic, peeled and minced
Salt and pepper, to taste
Grated Pecorino Romano cheese, for serving

1. *Bring a large pot of salted water to a boil. Add the pasta and cook according to package directions, or until al dente.*
2. *Cook the broccoli according to the package directions and drain.*
3. *Heat the oil in a saucepan over medium heat, and sauté the onion, tarragon, and garlic until the onion is slightly golden. Add the broccoli and salt and pepper to taste. Heat the broccoli through, remove from the heat, and stir in the pasta. Sprinkle with the cheese and serve.*

Penne with Basil Pesto, Tomatoes, & String Beans

4 to 6 servings

1 pound penne pasta
1/4 cup Pesto Sauce (see page 137), or to taste
1 cup chopped tomatoes
1 cup chopped, blanched green beans (see Box on page 66)
Grated Parmesan cheese, for serving
Salt and pepper, to taste

1. *Bring a large pot of salted water to a boil. Add the pasta and cook according to package directions, or until al dente.*
2. *Drain the pasta and place in a large bowl. Toss with the Pesto Sauce, tomatoes, and green beans. Add the Parmesan cheese and toss to incorporate. Season with salt and pepper to taste, and serve.*

Broccoli Rice

6 to 8 servings

1 tablespoon peanut oil
1/4 cup coarsely chopped peanuts
2-1/4 cups chopped broccoli florets
2 tablespoons chopped green onion
1 tablespoon minced garlic
1 cup chicken broth
2 tablespoons sherry or white wine
1-1/2 tablespoons soy sauce
1 cup instant-cook rice

1. *Heat the oil in a saucepan and sauté the peanuts until golden. Transfer to a paper towel to drain.*
2. *Place the broccoli, green onion, and garlic in the hot pan and cook, stirring occasionally, for 3 to 4 minutes.*
3. *Add the broth, sherry, and soy sauce and bring to a boil. Stir in the rice, return to a boil, and remove from heat. Cover, and set aside for about 5 minutes. Fluff with a fork, transfer to a bowl, and garnish with the peanuts.*

Curried Rice with Shallots

4 to 6 servings

2 tablespoons butter or margarine
2 shallots, peeled and sliced into 1/4-inch pieces
1/2 teaspoon curry powder
Pinch ground nutmeg or mace
2 cups cooked brown rice, hot
1/2 cup half-and-half or rice milk
Salt and pepper, to taste

Melt the butter in a saucepan and sauté the shallots until translucent. Add the curry and nutmeg, then stir in the rice, half-and-half, and salt and pepper to taste. Heat through and serve immediately.

Herbed Orange Rice

6 to 8 servings

1/4 cup butter or margarine

2/3 cup chopped celery, with greens

2 tablespoons minced white onion

1-1/2 cups unsweetened apple juice

1 tablespoon grated orange zest

1 cup orange juice

Pinch crushed dried tarragon

1 cup long grain rice

1. *Melt the butter in a saucepan and sauté the celery and onion until the onion is translucent.*
2. *Add the apple juice, orange zest, orange juice, and tarragon and bring to a boil. Add the rice, reduce to a low simmer, and cook for about 15 minutes, or until the rice is tender and all of the liquid is absorbed. Transfer to a bowl, fluff with a fork, and serve immediately.*

Red & Green Rice

6 to 8 servings

1 tablespoon extra virgin olive oil

1/4 cup chopped green bell pepper

1/4 cup sliced zucchini

4 cups cooked rice, hot

1/4 cup sliced green onion, with tops

1 (4 ounce) can pimiento, drained and chopped

2 tablespoons butter or margarine

Salt and pepper, to taste

Chopped fresh parsley, for garnish

1. *Heat the olive oil in a saucepan over medium heat. Add the green pepper and zucchini and sauté until tender.*
2. *In a bowl, combine the green pepper, zucchini, rice, green onion, pimiento, and butter, and toss gently. Add salt and pepper to taste, sprinkle with the chopped parsley, and serve immediately.*

Vegetable Rice Ring

4 to 6 servings

Rice Ring with Basil & Almonds

6 to 8 servings

Vegetable oil, for greasing the mold
6 cups cooked rice, hot
1/4 cup chopped fresh basil
1/4 cup butter or margarine, halved
1/4 cup chopped almonds

1. *Thoroughly grease a 5-1/2 cup ring mold.*
2. *In a large bowl, toss together 3 cups of the rice, the chopped basil, and half the butter. Using a serving spoon, press the mixture into the prepared mold.*
3. *In the same bowl, combine the remaining 3 cups rice, almonds, and remaining butter. Spoon into the ring mold and press firmly.*
4. *Immediately invert the ring mold onto a platter, and tap gently on the bottom of the mold to unmold the rice. The ring can be decorated using almost any combination of fruits or vegetables.*

This dish can be served hot or cold, with a variety of sauces on the side.

Vegetable oil, for greasing the mold
3/4 cup basmati rice
1 cup frozen chopped mixed vegetables, thawed
2 tablespoons extra virgin olive oil
1 tablespoon red wine vinegar
Salt and pepper, to taste
1/4 cup finely diced cheddar cheese
1 cup finely diced, cored, peeled, and seeded pears
1 fennel bulb, trimmed, and chopped, greens chopped and reserved for garnish
3 tablespoons sour cream or plain yogurt

1. *Use the vegetable oil to thoroughly grease a 6-cup ring mold.*
2. *Cook the rice according to the package directions and add the mixed vegetables during the last 5 minutes.*
3. *Drain the rice and vegetables and place in a bowl. Add the olive oil, vinegar, and salt and pepper to taste. Using a serving spoon, press the mixture into the ring mold.*
4. *In another bowl, combine the cheese, pears, and fennel. Fold in the sour cream, and salt and pepper to taste.*
5. *Immediately invert the ring mold onto a platter, and gently tap the bottom of the mold to unmold the rice.*
6. *Spoon the cheese and pear mixture into the center of the rice ring, and garnish with the chopped fennel greens.*
7. *Gently cover with plastic wrap and refrigerate for at least 1 hour before serving.*

Confetti Barley

6 to 8 servings

1/2 cup Italian dressing

1 cup sliced, stemmed seeded red bell pepper

1/2 cup chopped yellow onion

1 cup pearl barley

1-3/4 cups chicken broth

1-1/4 cups water or apple juice

2 tablespoons snipped fresh parsley

1 tablespoon fresh lime juice

1/2 teaspoon ground cumin

Salt and pepper, to taste

1 (7 ounce) can lima beans or whole kernel corn, drained

1. *Heat the dressing in a saucepan over medium heat. Add the pepper and onion and sauté until tender. Add the barley and cook, stirring until the barley is well coated with dressing.*
2. *Add the broth, water, parsley, lime juice, and cumin and bring to a boil. Reduce to a simmer, cover, and continue to cook without stirring or removing the cover, about 45 to 50 minutes.*
3. *Remove from the heat, fluff with a fork, stir in the limas or corn, and serve.*

Backyard Bakery

Afternoon Tea

SIPS AND STARTERS

•

Minted Ginger Tea
Honey Apple Tea
Cucumber & Radish Tea Sandwiches
Roast Beef & Horseradish Cream Sandwiches

SALADS

•

Watercress & Carrot Salad

ENTREES

•

Grilled Salmon Steaks with Lemon Herb Rub
Mykonos-Style Grilled Sliced Eggplant

SIDES

•

Savory Grilled Tomatoes
Creamy Spinach Casserole

FROM THE BAKERY

•

Baking Soda Biscuits
Soft Gingerbread Cake

Herbed Tomato Bread

1 loaf

Oil or shortening, for greasing the pan

3 cups all-purpose flour

2-1/2 teaspoons baking powder

1/2 teaspoon baking soda

2 tablespoons snipped fresh tarragon

1 tablespoon snipped fresh parsley

1 tablespoon granulated sugar

1 cup finely grated cheddar cheese

1/2 teaspoon salt

2 large eggs

1 cup milk

1/4 cup canola oil

2 tablespoons tomato paste

1 small yellow onion, finely chopped

1 teaspoon ketchup

1/2 cup grated provolone cheese, for topping

1. *Position a rack in the center of the oven and preheat to 350° F. Lightly grease and flour a 9-1/4- x 5-1/4- x 2-3/4-inch loaf pan.*
2. *In a large bowl, blend together the flour, baking powder, baking soda, tarragon, parsley, sugar, cheddar cheese, and salt.*
3. *In a medium bowl, beat the eggs until foamy, then beat in the milk, oil, tomato paste, onion, and ketchup. Combine the wet and dry mixtures until the dry ingredients are moistened.*
4. *Scrape the batter into the prepared pan and sprinkle the provolone cheese over the top. Bake for 55 to 60 minutes, until the top is golden and a wooden toothpick inserted into the center of the bread comes out clean. Remove the bread from the oven and cool on a wire rack for 5 to 10 minutes before removing the bread from the pan.*

Pepper and Feta Bread

1 loaf

Oil or shortening, for greasing the pan

1 medium red bell pepper, stemmed, seeded, and finely chopped

1 medium yellow bell pepper, stemmed, seeded, and finely chopped

1 tablespoon olive oil

2-1/2 cups all-purpose flour

1-1/4 teaspoons baking powder

1/4 teaspoon baking soda

1/4 teaspoon salt

1 tablespoon snipped fresh rosemary

1/2 cup crumbled feta cheese

3 tablespoons melted butter or margarine

1 large egg

1-1/4 cups milk

Salt and freshly ground black pepper, to taste

1. *Position a rack in the center of the oven and preheat to 350° F. Lightly grease and flour a 9-1/4- x 5-1/4- x 2-3/4-inch loaf pan.*
2. *In a medium skillet set over a medium heat, sauté the peppers in the olive oil until tender. Set aside.*
3. *In a large bowl, blend together the flour, baking powder, baking soda, salt, rosemary, and cheese. In a small bowl beat together the butter and egg until smooth before beating in the milk. Stir in the cooked peppers. Combine the two mixtures, blending until the dry ingredients are thoroughly moistened. Add salt and pepper to taste.*
4. *Scrape the batter into the prepared baking pan and bake for 55 to 60 minutes, or until a wooden toothpick inserted into the center of the bread comes out clean and the top is golden. Remove from the oven and cool on a wire rack for 5 to 10 minutes before removing the bread from the pan.*

Focaccia

About 12 servings

Oil or shortening, for greasing the baking sheet

2-3/4 cups all-purpose flour

1 teaspoon salt

1 teaspoon granulated sugar

1 tablespoon active dry yeast

1 teaspoon garlic powder

Pinch black pepper

3 tablespoons olive oil, plus more for oiling the bowl

1 cup warm water

Fresh rosemary leaves, optional

1/4 cup grated Parmesan cheese, optional

1. *In a large bowl, stir together the flour, salt, sugar, yeast, garlic powder, and pepper. Add 1 tablespoon of the olive oil and the warm water and stir until a dough forms.*
2. *Turn the dough out onto a lightly floured surface and knead until smooth and elastic. Lightly coat a large bowl with olive oil, place the dough in the bowl, and turn it to coat with the oil. Cover the dough with a damp cloth, and set in a warm place to rise for 20 minutes.*
3. *Meanwhile, preheat the oven to 450° F. When the dough has risen, punch it down and place it on a greased baking sheet. Shape it into a 1/2-inch thick rectangle and brush the top with the remaining olive oil. Sprinkle with the rosemary and Parmesan cheese, if desired.*
4. *Place in the oven and bake for 15 minutes, or until golden brown.*

Pecan-Raisin Sorghum Bread

2 loaves

Oil or shortening, for greasing the pan

1 cup granulated sugar

4 tablespoons unsalted butter, melted

2 large eggs

1 cup buttermilk

2/3 cup sorghum

1 cup chopped pecans or walnuts

1 cup all-purpose flour

1 teaspoon salt

1 teaspoon baking powder

1 teaspoon baking soda

2 cups graham flour

1 cup chopped seedless raisins

1. *Position a rack in the center of the oven and preheat to 350° F. Lightly grease two 8- x 4-inch loaf baking pans.*

2. *In a bowl, use a whisk or electric mixer to beat the sugar and butter until the sugar is dissolved. Beat in the eggs, one at a time, until incorporated. Add the buttermilk and sorghum and beat vigorously for 1 or 2 minutes.*

3. *In a second bowl, combine the nuts, flour, salt, baking powder, baking soda, graham flour, and raisins. Fold into the moist mixture, until just moistened. Spoon equally into the prepared baking pans, and bake for about 50 to 60 minutes, or until a toothpick inserted into the center of the bread comes out clean. Remove from the oven, cool on a wire rack for about 5 minutes, then invert onto a plate and remove the loaf from the pan before serving.*

Spoonbread

8 to 10 servings

Oil or shortening, for greasing the pan

1-1/2 cups water

1 cup corn meal

1 tablespoon granulated sugar

1 teaspoon salt

1-1/2 teaspoons baking powder

3 tablespoons butter or margarine, at room temperature

1-1/2 cups milk

3 large eggs, separated

1. *Position a rack in the center of the oven and preheat to 325° F. Lightly grease a 9- x 9- x 2-inch baking dish.*
2. *Place the water in a saucepan, bring to a boil, and add the corn meal all at once, stirring constantly until mushy and thick.*
3. *Remove from the heat and stir in the sugar, salt, baking powder, and butter, until blended. Stir in the milk, until incorporated. Beat in the egg yolks.*
4. *In a bowl, use a whisk or electric mixer to beat the egg whites stiff, but not dry. Fold into the mixture, and pour into the prepared baking pan. Bake for 50 to 55 minutes, or until a toothpick inserted into the center of the bread comes out clean. Remove from the oven and serve.*

Sour Cream-Chive Crescent Rolls

About 40 rolls

1 cup sour cream

1 teaspoon salt

1/2 cup granulated sugar

1/2 cup unsalted butter, melted

2 packages active dry yeast

1/2 cup warm water

2 eggs

4 cups all-purpose flour

1/4 cup snipped fresh chives

Oil or shortening, for greasing the baking sheets

1. *In a small pan heat the sour cream until very hot but not boiling. Add the salt, sugar, and melted butter and remove from the heat. Let cool to lukewarm.*
2. *In a large bowl, dissolve the yeast in the warm water. Stir in the sour cream mixture, eggs, flour, and chives. Cover and place in the refrigerator overnight.*
3. *Divide the dough into 4 equal parts, and knead and roll each part into a 10-inch circle. Cut each circle into 10 narrow wedges, and roll up each wedge from the base to the point. Place the rolls on greased baking sheets and let them rise until double in size. Preheat the oven to 375° F.*
4. *Place the rolls in the oven and bake for 12 to 15 minutes, or until golden.*

Tea for Two . . . or More: Tea Party Invitations

Planning to host a tea party anytime soon? The alluring invitation is an essential. For traditional tea parties, invitations should be received two weeks prior to the date, and should include date, time, address, telephone number, directions or map, and "regrets only by," with a date set for responses. Once you have all the information ready for your invitation, decide how you want to present it to your guests. Invitations can be designed to match the formality or theme of your gathering.

Depending on your budget, invitations can range from expensive engraved cards, to printed cards from a card store, to more affordable plain announcements. You can use the occasion as a good opportunity to practice your calligraphy skills and add an elegant, yet homemade, touch to invitations. Or use a word processing program on your home computer to see different fonts and layouts. Another way to liven up an invite is to write it in the form of a limerick or poem to suit the theme of the party. You could even cut your invitation into the shape of a teacup or something else related to your theme. Finally, you can put a cyber spin on the tea-party tradition with an E-mail invite.

Baking Soda Biscuits

10 to 12 servings

Oil or shortening, for greasing the baking sheet
2 cups all-purpose flour
1/2 teaspoon baking soda
1/2 teaspoon salt
4 tablespoons vegetable shortening
3/4 cup buttermilk

1. *Position a rack in the center of the oven and preheat to 350° F. Lightly grease a baking sheet.*
2. *In a bowl, combine the flour, soda, and salt. Using a pastry knife or two knives, cut in the shortening until the mixture resembles a fine crumb. Make a well in the center of the mixture, and add the buttermilk, working from the side, and blend to make a soft, sticky dough.*
3. *Turn out onto a lightly floured surface, sprinkle very lightly with flour, and knead for about 1 minute. Using a rolling pin, roll out to a thickness of 1/2 inch, and cut into rounds. Arrange the rounds on the prepared baking sheet, and bake for 10 to 12 minutes, or until the biscuits are a very light golden color. Remove from the oven, keep warm, and serve.*

The old-fashioned way to cut circles: Use a drinking glass dipped in flour.

Buttermilk Biscuits

10 to 12 biscuits

2 cups all-purpose flour
2-1/2 teaspoons baking powder
1/4 teaspoon baking soda
1 tablespoon granulated sugar
1/4 teaspoon salt
6 tablespoons butter or margarine, chilled
3/4 cup buttermilk
1/4 cup melted butter or margarine (for brushing)

1. *Position a rack in the center of the oven and preheat to 425° F.*
2. *In a large bowl, blend together the flour, baking powder, baking soda, sugar, and salt. Using a pastry blender or two knives, cut in the chilled butter until the mixture resembles fine meal. Add the buttermilk all at once and stir just until the dough holds together (be careful not to overmix).*
3. *Turn the dough out onto a lightly floured surface and knead 7 or 8 times. Using a rolling pin, roll the dough out to a thickness of 1/2 inch. Using a 2-inch round cutter or the top of a cup or glass, cut out as many biscuits as possible. Place the biscuits 1 inch apart on an ungreased baking sheet. Rework the scraps until all the dough is used. Brush with the melted butter, and bake for 10 to 12 minutes or until the tops of the biscuits are golden brown. Serve warm.*

Jalapeño Cheddar Biscuits

6 biscuits

1 cup all-purpose flour

2 tablespoons corn meal

1-1/2 teaspoons baking powder

1/2 cup finely grated sharp cheddar cheese, or other sharp cheese

2 tablespoons peeled, seeded, and chopped tomato

1 teaspoon stemmed, seeded, and minced jalapeño pepper

1/2 teaspoon salt

1/2 cup milk

1. *Position a rack in the center of the oven and preheat to 425° F.*
2. *In a large bowl, blend together the flour, corn meal, baking powder, cheese, tomato, jalapeño pepper, and salt. Add the milk all at once and stir just until the dough holds together (be careful not to overmix).*
3. *Turn the dough out onto a lightly floured surface and knead 7 or 8 times. Divide the dough into 6 equal balls and place the balls on an ungreased baking sheet. Pat the balls into 3-inch rounds. Bake for 10 to 12 minutes, or until the tops of the biscuits are golden brown. Serve warm.*

A Bit About Biscuits

Biscuit comes from the French words *bis* and *cuit*, which together mean "cooked twice." Biscuits aboard ships were originally cooked twice to regain their crispness before being eaten by sailors on the high seas.

English Cream Scones

10 to 12 scones

2 cups all-purpose flour

1 tablespoon baking powder

4 teaspoons granulated sugar, plus more for sprinkling
over the scones

1/2 teaspoon salt

1/4 cup chilled butter or margarine, diced

2 large eggs, beaten

1/2 cup sweet cream

1 cup black currants, plumped in hot water and drained

1 beaten egg white

1. *Position the rack in the center of the oven and preheat to 375 ° F. Lightly grease and flour a baking sheet.*

2. *In a large bowl, blend together the flour, baking powder, 4 teaspoons of the sugar, and the salt. Using a pastry blender or two knives, cut in the butter until the mixture resembles coarse meal. Add the eggs, cream, and currants, stirring gently until the dough holds together.*

3. *Turn the dough out onto a floured surface and knead several times before rolling out to a thickness of 1/2 inch. Using a biscuit cutter, cut the dough into 2-inch circles, reworking the scraps as you go.*

4. *Place the circles 1-inch apart on the prepared baking sheet. Brush with the beaten egg white and sprinkle with the remaining sugar. Bake for 15 to 18 minutes, or until golden brown. Remove from the oven and serve hot with butter or whipped cream (see page 215) and jam.*

Chocolate Raspberry Muffins

12 to 14 muffins

Oil or shortening, for greasing muffin cups

2 cups all-purpose flour

2 teaspoons baking powder

1/2 teaspoon baking soda

1/2 cup granulated sugar

6 ounces semisweet chocolate, finely chopped

1 large egg

2 tablespoons butter or margarine, melted

3/4 cup buttermilk

1 cup raspberry preserves

Finely chopped pecans, for top (optional)

1. *Position a rack in the center of the oven and preheat to 375° F. Lightly grease 14 muffin cups or line with paper baking cups.*

2. *In a large bowl, blend together the flour, baking powder, baking soda, sugar, and chocolate. In a medium bowl, beat together the egg, butter, and buttermilk until smooth. Combine the dry and wet ingredients, mixing until the dry ingredients are just moistened. Using a rubber spatula, gently fold in the raspberry preserves.*

3. *Spoon the batter into muffin cups, filling each about three-quarters full. Sprinkle with chopped pecans and bake for about 12 to 15 minutes, or until a wooden toothpick inserted into the center of a muffin comes out clean. Cool in the pan on a wire rack for about 5 minutes and serve warm, or invert onto the rack to cool completely.*

The Royal Highland Muffin

About 16 servings

Oil or shortening, for greasing the muffin cups

1-2/3 cups all-purpose flour

2-1/2 teaspoons baking powder

1/2 teaspoon salt

1/2 cup plus 2 tablespoons butter or margarine, softened

1/2 cup sugar

2 large eggs, beaten

1-1/4 cups heavy cream

3/4 cup wheat germ

1 cup dried red currants

1. *Position a rack in the center of the oven and preheat to 375° F. Lightly grease 16 muffin cups.*

2. *In a bowl, combine the flour, baking powder, and salt.*

3. *In a second bowl, using a electric mixer, beat the butter until light and fluffy. Vigorously beat in the sugar and egg until blended. Then, alternating, add the dry ingredients and the heavy cream, until just blended. Fold in the wheat germ and currants.*

4. *Spoon the batter into the prepared muffin cups, filling each cup about two-thirds full.*

5. *Bake for about 15 to 20 minutes, or until a toothpick inserted into the center of the muffins comes out clean. Remove from the oven, cool slightly, and serve.*

Raspberry Almond Muffins

12 muffins

Oil or shortening, for greasing muffin cups
2-1/2 cups all-purpose flour
1 tablespoon baking powder
1-1/2 cups raspberries, rinsed and dried
1 cup slivered almonds
2 tablespoons poppy seeds
1/2 teaspoon salt
2 large eggs
1/2 cup granulated sugar
1 cup milk
3 tablespoons butter or vegetable shortening, melted

1. *Position the rack in the center of the oven and preheat to 375° F. Lightly grease 12 muffin cups or line with paper baking cups.*
2. *In a large bowl, stir together the flour, baking powder, raspberries, almonds, poppy seeds, and salt. In a medium bowl, beat the eggs until foamy. Beat in the sugar, milk and butter. Combine the two mixtures, blending until the dry ingredients are just moistened.*
3. *Spoon the batter into the prepared muffin cups, filling each about three-quarters full. Bake for 15 to 20 minutes, or until a wooden toothpick inserted in the center of a muffin comes out clean. Cool in the pan on a wire rack for 5 to 7 minutes, and serve warm, or invert onto the rack to cool completely.*

Soft Gingerbread Cake

10 to 16 servings

Oil or shortening, for greasing the pan

3-2/3 cups flour

1-1/2 teaspoons baking soda

1/4 teaspoon salt

1 teaspoon ground cinnamon

1 teaspoon ground cloves

1 teaspoon ground ginger

1/4 teaspoon ground nutmeg

1/2 cup vegetable shortening

2/3 cup granulated sugar

1 large egg

2/3 cup molasses

1-1/4 cups boiling water

Sweetened Whipped Cream (see page 213)

   or vanilla ice cream, for serving

1. *Position a rack in the center of the oven and preheat to 375° F. Lightly grease a 9-inch baking pan.*
2. *Combine the flour, baking soda, salt, cinnamon, cloves, ginger, and nutmeg and set aside.*
3. *In a bowl, cream together the shortening and sugar until fluffy. Beat in the egg.*
4. *In a separate bowl, whisk together the molasses and water. Alternating with the dry ingredients, beat the molasses mixture into the egg mixture until just smooth. Pour into the prepared baking pan, and bake for 40 to 45 minutes, or until the cake pulls away from the sides.*
5. *Remove from the oven and let cool on a wire rack. When ready, cut into squares and serve with Sweetened Whipped Cream or a scoop of vanilla ice cream.*

Cinnamon Coffee Cake

8 to 10 servings

Topping

1/2 cup firmly packed brown sugar

1/2 cup finely chopped walnuts

2 tablespoons all-purpose flour

2 teaspoons ground cinnamon

2 tablespoons canola oil

Batter

1-1/2 cups all-purpose flour

1/2 cup granulated sugar

2-1/2 teaspoons baking powder

1/2 teaspoon salt

1 large egg white

1/4 cup canola oil

3/4 cup milk

1. *Position a rack in the center of the oven and preheat to 375° F. Lightly grease and flour the bottom of an 8-inch baking pan.*
2. *In a small bowl combine the topping ingredients and mix until crumbly.*
3. *In a large bowl, blend together the flour, sugar, baking powder, and salt. In a medium bowl, beat the egg white until foamy and beat in the oil and milk. Combine the wet and dry ingredients, blending until the dry ingredients are moistened.*
4. *Spoon half of the batter into the prepared baking pan and top with half of the topping. Spoon the remaining batter into the pan and top with the remaining topping. Bake for 30 to 35 minutes, or until a toothpick inserted into the center of the cake comes out clean. Remove the pan from the oven and cool on a wire rack for 5 to 7 minutes. Serve warm or cool.*

Rich Buttercream Frosting

Great Aunt Ida's Easy Yellow Cake with Rich Buttercream Frosting

About 12 servings

Oil or shortening, for greasing the pan
1-1/2 cups all-purpose flour
1 cup granulated sugar
2 teaspoons baking powder
1/2 teaspoon salt
3/4 cup milk
1/3 cup butter or margarine, cubed
1 large egg
2 teaspoons vanilla extract
Rich Buttercream Frosting (recipe follows)

1. *Position a rack in the center of the oven and preheat to 350° F. Lightly grease and flour an 8-inch square pan or cupcake tins.*

2. *In a bowl, combine all of the ingredients and beat together with an electric mixer on medium speed until smooth, about 3 minutes.*

3. *Pour into the prepared baking pan, and bake for 30 to 35 minutes (15 to 12 minutes for cupcakes), or until a toothpick inserted into the center comes out clean. Remove from the oven and let cool in the pan on a wire rack for about 10 minutes before cutting. If the cake is to be frosted, cool completely in the pan, and frost with Rich Buttercream Frosting.*

1 (16 ounce) package confectioners' sugar
6 tablespoons butter or margarine, at room temperature
3 to 4 tablespoons evaporated milk
1-1/2 teaspoons vanilla extract
Food coloring, if desired

In a bowl, combine the sugar, butter, evaporated milk, and vanilla extract. Using an electric mixer on high speed, beat until smooth. Add additional milk as needed to make a good spreading consistency, and food coloring, if desired. Spread on a cooled cake, cupcakes, or other baked items.

Variations

LEMON: *Substitute fresh lemon juice for the evaporated milk, and omit the vanilla extract, or use triple sec liqueur in its place.*

MOCHA: *Add 1/2 cup cocoa powder and substitute 1/3 cup hot coffee for the evaporated milk and amaretto liqueur for the vanilla extract.*

ORANGE: *1 teaspoon grated orange zest.*

CHOCOLATE: *Increase the butter to 1/2 cup and add 3 squares melted unsweetened chocolate.*

Cherry Chocolate Cupcakes

16 to 18 cupcakes

Oil or shortening, for greasing the cupcake tins
1/2 cup butter or margarine, at room temperature
1 cup granulated sugar
1 teaspoon pure vanilla extract
4 large eggs
1-1/2 cups all-purpose flour
3/4 teaspoon baking soda
1 (16 ounce) can chocolate syrup
1/2 cup diced dried cherries
Chocolate Fudge Frosting (recipe follows)

1. *Position a rack in the center of the oven and preheat to 375° F. Lightly grease 18 cupcake tins or line with paper baking cups.*
2. *In a bowl, using an electric mixer, beat together the butter, sugar, and vanilla extract until fluffy. Beat in the eggs one at a time, beating vigorously after each addition.*
3. *In a second bowl, stir together the flour and baking soda.*
4. *Combine the wet and dry ingredients, alternating with the chocolate syrup, until the dry ingredients are just incorporated. Fold in the cherry pieces and spoon into the prepared cupcake tins, filling each cup about three-quarters full.*
5. *Bake for about 15 to 20 minutes, or until a toothpick inserted into the center of the cupcake comes out clean. Remove the cupcake tins from the oven and cool on a wire rack for 10 minutes before removing the cupcakes from the baking pan. Frost if desired.*

Chocolate Fudge Frosting

4 ounces unsweetened chocolate, grated or finely chopped
3 cups confectioners' sugar, sifted
4 teaspoons light corn syrup
1/2 cup heavy cream
3 tablespoons boiling water
4 teaspoons butter or margarine, at room temperature
2 teaspoons chocolate extract

1. *Melt the chocolate in a double boiler and place in a large bowl.*
2. *Using an electric mixer on low, beat in the confectioners' sugar and corn syrup. Blend in the cream and boiling water. Add the butter and chocolate extract and beat until a spreadable consistency. Chill for 30 minutes before using.*

Mock Angel Food Cake

12 to 16 servings

1/2 unsliced loaf white sandwich bread
1 (14 ounce) can sweetened condensed milk
2 (3-1/2 ounce) cans sweetened flaked coconut

1. *Using a sharp knife, remove the crust from the bread and cut the bread into 3/4-inch slices. Dip each slice in the condensed milk and dredge in the coconut.*
2. *Place the slices on a warm grill, and cook for about 10 minutes, turning frequently, until toasted. Remove from the grill and serve warm.*

Barbecued Pound Cake

6 to 8 servings

1 (8 ounce) frozen pound cake
4 tablespoons butter or margarine, at room temperature
2 cups fresh strawberries, rinsed, hulled, and sliced
Sweetened Whipped Cream (see page 213)

Thaw the pound cake slightly and cut into slices. Butter both sides of each piece, and arrange on a warm grill. Toast for about 2 minutes on each side, or until just golden brown. Transfer to serving plates, and spoon strawberries over each slice. Garnish with a dollop of Sweetened Whipped Cream and serve.

If frozen pound cake is not available, regular pound cake can be used—simply freeze it and thaw it slightly before placing on the grill.

Festive Party Favors

A small gift given to a guest or used as ornamentation, a favor can spruce up the party guests, as well as the ambiance. For a tea, consider some of the classier favors: miniature porcelain teapots or miniature baskets filled with cheeses. Provide favors to correspond to your theme. If you're going for French country, hang some artificial vines and foliage along the walls, and offer bowls of fresh grapes. There is an endless selection of manufactured favors at your local party supply store as well: bows, ribbons, gift wrap, tissue paper, confetti, streamers, Mylar and helium balloons, decorative plates, napkins, cups, candles, funny hats . . . you get the idea.

Apple Cobbler

4 to 6 servings

World's Easiest Apple Pie

One 10-inch pie

FILLING

1 cup granulated sugar

1/4 cup all-purpose flour

1/4 teaspoon ground cinnamon

6 cups peeled, cored, and sliced apples

TOPPING

1 cup all-purpose flour

1/4 cup granulated sugar

1-1/2 teaspoons baking powder

1/2 teaspoon salt

1-1/2 cups shredded cheddar cheese

1/3 cup melted butter or margarine

1/4 cup milk

1. *Position a rack in the center of the oven and preheat to 400° F. Lightly grease and flour the bottom of a 9-inch baking pan or chaffing dish.*
2. *To make the filling, in a plastic bag combine the sugar, flour, cinnamon, and apples and shake to coat. Spread evenly into the prepared baking pan.*
3. *To make the topping, in a large bowl combine the flour, sugar, baking powder, salt, and cheese. Stir in the butter and milk until the dry ingredients are just moistened, and spread over the top of the apple mixture in the pan.*
4. *Bake for 28 to 30 minutes, or until the topping is golden brown. Cool in the pan on a wire rack for 5 to 7 minutes. Serve warm.*

Oil or shortening, for greasing the pan

2 cups sliced apples

1 tablespoon fresh lemon juice

1/2 cup plus 2 tablespoons biscuit baking mix

1-1/2 cups water or apple juice

3 large eggs

1 (14 ounce) can sweetened condensed milk

1/4 cup butter or margarine, at room temperature

1-1/2 teaspoons almond extract

1/2 teaspoon ground cinnamon

1/2 teaspoon ground nutmeg

Vanilla ice cream, for serving (optional)

1. *Position a rack in the center of the oven and preheat to 350° F. Lightly grease the bottom of a 10-inch pie tin.*
2. *In a bowl, combine the apples and lemon juice, tossing gently until coated. Sprinkle on 2 tablespoons of the biscuit baking mix, and arrange in the bottom of the prepared pie tin.*
3. *In a blender, combine the water and eggs and process on high until smooth. Add the remaining baking mix, condensed milk, butter, almond extract, cinnamon, and nutmeg and process on low for 2 to 3 minutes. Carefully pour over the apple slices.*
4. *Place the pie in the oven and bake for about 35 to 40 minutes, or until the top is lightly colored and golden brown around the edges. Remove from the oven and serve immediately with vanilla ice cream, if desired.*

Chocolate Cream Pie

One 9-inch pie

CRUST

1-1/2 cups finely crushed graham crackers

1/3 cup butter, melted

3 tablespoons sugar

FILLING

4 large egg yolks

1-1/2 cups granulated sugar

1/3 cup cornstarch

1/2 teaspoon salt

3 cups milk

2 ounces unsweetened baking chocolate, chopped

Banana slices, Sweetened Whipped Cream (see page 213),
   and shaved chocolate, for garnish

1. To make the pie crust, in a bowl, combine the graham crackers,
   butter, and sugar and cut together until the mixture is a coarse
   crumb. Press into a 9-inch pie tin and bake for about 10 minutes in a 350° F oven, or until light brown. Remove from the
   oven and set aside.
2. Position a rack in the center of the oven and preheat to 425° F.
3. To make the filling, in a medium bowl beat the egg yolks with a
   fork and set aside. In a saucepan, mix together the sugar, cornstarch, and salt. Slowly stir in the milk and chocolate and cook
   over medium heat, stirring constantly, until the chocolate melts
   and the mixture thickens and boils. Boil, stirring, for 1 minute.
4. Stir half of the hot chocolate mixture into the eggs to temper
   them, then stir the heated yolk mixture back into the chocolate
   mixture. Bring to a boil and cook for 1 minute. Remove from the
   heat, and stir in the vanilla.

5. Pour the filling into the prepared pie crust and coat the surface
   with plastic wrap to prevent a skin from forming on the filling.
   Refrigerate for at least 2 hours, or until set. Before serving,
   remove the plastic and garnish with banana slices, Sweetened
   Whipped Cream, and shaved chocolate, if desired.

Chocolate Peanut Butter Pie

One 9-inch pie

1-1/2 cups chocolate wafer crumbs (about 30 wafers crushed)

3/4 cup granulated sugar

1/2 cup butter, melted

1 cup chunky peanut butter

1 (8 ounce) package cream cheese, at room temperature

1/4 cup butter

1 teaspoon vanilla extract

2 cups heavy cream

1/4 cup chopped peanuts

1. *Preheat the oven to 350° F. To make the crust, combine the wafer crumbs, 1/4 cup of the sugar, and the melted butter. Press into the bottom of a 9-inch springform pan and bake for 8 minutes. Remove and let cool.*
2. *For the filling, beat together the peanut butter, cream cheese, 1/4 cup butter, remaining 1/2 cup sugar, and vanilla extract. In a separate bowl, whip 1 cup of the cream until it forms soft peaks. Fold into the peanut butter mixture and heap onto crust. Cover and refrigerate for at least 2 hours.*
3. *Just before serving, whip the remaining cup of cream until it forms soft peaks, and remove the sides of the springform pan. Spread the whipped cream over the top of the pie and garnish with the chopped peanuts.*

Fluffy Orange Pie

One 9-inch pie

2 cups vanilla wafer crumbs

1/3 cup melted butter or margarine

1 (8 ounce) package cream cheese, at room temperature

1 (14 ounce) can sweetened condensed milk

1 (6 ounce) can frozen orange juice concentrate, thawed

1 (8 ounce) container heavy cream, whipped

Fresh or candied orange slices, for garnish (optional)

1. *In a bowl, using your hands, mix together the wafer crumbs and butter until incorporated. Press into the bottom of a 9-inch pie tin, and refrigerate for at least 2 hours, or until needed.*
2. *Meanwhile, in a bowl, use a whisk or electric mixer to beat the cream cheese smooth and fluffy. Slowly beat in the condensed milk and orange juice until smooth. Fold in the whipped cream, heap the mixture into the chilled pie crust, and place in the coldest section of the refrigerator for at least 2 hours or until set. Garnish with fresh or candied orange slices, and serve.*

Mississippi Mud Pie

8 to 10 servings

20 chocolate sandwich cookies, finely crushed

3 tablespoons butter or margarine, melted

2 pints coffee ice cream, softened

1 cup hot fudge sauce, at room temperature

1/4 cup chopped toffee or toasted almonds, for topping

1. *In a large bowl, mix together the cookie crumbs and butter until well incorporated. Press into a 9-inch pie pan to create a crust. Bake in a 350° F oven for about 10 minutes. Let cool.*
2. *Spread the ice cream into the crust and place in the freezer for 1 hour, or until firm enough to be topped with the fudge sauce.*
3. *Spread the hot fudge sauce over the ice cream and sprinkle with the toffee or almonds. Place in the freezer for at least 2 hours, then let sit out of the freezer for a few minutes before serving.*

SWEETENED WHIPPED CREAM

2 cups

1 cup heavy cream

2 tablespoons granulated or confectioners' sugar

In a medium chilled bowl, beat the cream and sugar with an electric mixer on high until soft peaks form. You can flavor whipped cream by adding an additional teaspoon of sugar and any flavoring you wish, such as one of the following:

1 teaspoon vanilla extract

1 teaspoon grated citrus zest

1/2 teaspoon ground cinnamon

1 teaspoon cocoa powder

1 teaspoon ground ginger

Teas for All Tastebuds

Although we declared independence from England more than two centuries ago, some habits, like tea-totalling, die hard. Tea is still very much a part of North American culture. There are a number of different teas to serve—green, yellow, white, oolongs, black, blends, scented, and more. Tea gurus offer these words of wisdom: Do not steep tea in individual cups. Teapots are better at retaining the aroma and flavor that would otherwise escape, and loose tease are always more enticing than bagged.

Butterscotch Bars

1 to 2 dozen

CRUST

3/4 cup butterscotch chips

1/3 cup butter, at room temperature

2 cups graham cracker crumbs

1 cup walnuts, finely ground

FILLING

1 (8 ounce) package cream cheese, at room temperature

1 (14 ounce) can sweetened condensed milk

1 large egg

1 teaspoon vanilla extract

1. *Preheat the oven to 350° F. Lightly grease a 13- x 9-inch baking pan.*
2. *To make the crust, melt the butterscotch chips and butter in a medium saucepan, stirring until smooth. Remove from the heat, pour into a large bowl, and blend in the graham cracker crumbs and walnuts. Spread half of this mixture evenly into the bottom of the prepared baking pan.*
3. *To make the filling, beat the cream cheese and condensed milk together in a small bowl. Beat in the egg and vanilla extract. Pour this mixture over the crust.*
4. *Spread the remaining crust mixture over the filling.*
5. *Bake for 25 to 30 minutes, or until a toothpick inserted in the center of the pan comes out clean. Cool in the pan on a wire rack before cutting into bars.*

Double Chocolate Brownies

12 servings

3/4 cup all-purpose flour

1/2 teaspoon baking powder

1/2 teaspoon salt

2 ounces unsweetened chocolate, grated or finely chopped

1/3 cup butter or margarine

1 cup granulated sugar

1 teaspoon vanilla extract

2 large eggs

1/2 cup chopped semisweet chocolate

1. *Position a rack in the center of the oven and preheat to 350° F. Lightly grease a 9-inch square baking pan.*
2. *Combine the flour, baking powder, and salt.*
3. *In the top of a double boiler, melt the chocolate and butter, stirring until smooth. Remove from the heat and place in a large bowl.*
4. *Using an electric mixer, beat in the sugar and vanilla extract. Beat in the eggs. Gradually blend in the dry ingredients. Fold in the chopped chocolate.*
4. *Scrape the batter into the prepared pan and spread evenly.*
5. *Bake for 30 to 35 minutes, or until a toothpick inserted into the center comes out clean. Cool in the pan on a wire rack before cutting.*

World's Best Chocolate Chip Cookies

6 to 7 dozen cookies

2-1/4 cups all-purpose flour
1 teaspoon baking soda
1 package vanilla-flavored instant pudding
1 cup vegetable shortening
1/4 cup granulated sugar
3/4 cup packed light brown sugar
2 large eggs
1 teaspoon vanilla extract
1-1/2 cups semisweet chocolate chips
1 cup walnuts, finely chopped (optional)

1. *Preheat the oven to 375° F.*
2. *Combine the flour, baking soda, and vanilla pudding mix.*
3. *In a large bowl, cream together the vegetable shortening and the two sugars. Beat in the eggs and the vanilla extract. Gradually blend in the dry ingredients. Fold in the chocolate chips and walnuts, if desired.*
4. *Drop the dough by spoonfuls 1-1/2 inches apart onto ungreased baking sheets.*
5. *Bake for 8 to 10 minutes, until lightly golden. Transfer to wire racks to cool.*

For chocolate-chocolate chip cookies, use chocolate instant pudding mix in place of the vanilla pudding.

Trail Mix Cookies

3 to 4 dozen cookies

Oil or shortening, for greasing the baking sheets
3/4 cup all-purpose flour
1/2 teaspoon baking soda
1/2 cup vegetable shortening
1 cup packed light brown sugar
1/2 cup peanut butter
1 large egg
1 teaspoon vanilla extract
1 cup semisweet chocolate chips
1 cup raisins
2/3 cup peanuts, chopped

1. *Preheat the oven to 375° F. Lightly grease 2 baking sheets.*
2. *Combine the flour and baking soda.*
3. *In a large bowl, cream the vegetable shortening and brown sugar. Beat in the peanut butter, egg, and vanilla extract. Fold in the chocolate chips, raisins, and peanuts.*
4. *Drop the dough by spoonfuls 1-1/2 inches apart onto the prepared baking sheets.*
5. *Bake for 10 to 12 minutes, until lightly golden. Transfer to wire racks to cool.*
6. *When the cookies are cool, wrap individually and store in an airtight container.*

Tracking Treasure

Understandably, kids get bored around large crowds of adults. An easy and fun solution to their young restlessness: Send them on a treasure hunt. Here are some ideas to help set them off searching:

*   *Fill small "treasure boxes"—metal containers like Altoid mint boxes work well— with small plastic jewels or little candies.*

*   *Place the treasures around the house or yard— under a pillow, beneath a hedge, nothing too difficult.*

*   *Split groups into a few teams but make sure there are enough "treasures" to be found by each.*

*   *Designate an adult for each team to help guide the tots along in the right direction. When the kids find the booty, the adults may reap some spoils of the hunt: the smiles of happy children.*

Jumbo Peanut Butter Cookies

2 to 3 dozen cookies

Oil or shortening, for greasing the baking sheets
2-1/2 cups all-purpose flour
1 teaspoon baking powder
1-1/2 teaspoons baking soda
2 cups packed light brown sugar
1 cup vegetable shortening
1 cup peanut butter
2 large eggs

1. *Preheat the oven to 350° F. Lightly grease 2 baking sheets.*
2. *Combine the flour, baking powder, and baking soda.*
3. *In a large bowl, beat together the brown sugar, vegetable shortening, peanut butter, and eggs. Gradually blend in the dry ingredients. The dough will be very soft.*
4. *Using a serving spoon, drop the dough by spoonfuls 3 inches apart onto the prepared baking sheets. Using the back of a fork dipped in flour, spread the cookies into large rounds.*
5. *Bake for 10 to 12 minutes, until golden brown. Cool on the baking sheets on wire racks.*

Chunky peanut butter can be used for cookies with more crunch.

Bird's Nest Cookies

3 to 4 dozen cookies

2 cups all-purpose flour
1/4 teaspoon salt
1 cup vegetable shortening
1/2 cup granulated sugar
1 large egg, separated
1 large egg yolk
1-1/2 teaspoons vanilla extract
1 cup walnuts, finely chopped
Chocolate kisses, for garnish

1. *Preheat the oven to 375° F.*
2. *Combine the flour and salt.*
3. *In a large bowl, cream the vegetable shortening and sugar. Beat in the 2 egg yolks and vanilla extract. Gradually blend in the flour mixture.*
4. *In a shallow bowl, beat the egg white until frothy.*
5. *Spread the walnuts on waxed paper.*
6. *Break off 1-inch pieces of the dough and roll into balls. Dip the balls in the egg white to coat, then roll in the walnuts and place 1 inch apart on ungreased baking sheets.*
7. *With your finger, make a small depression in the center of each cookie. Bake for 12 to 15 minutes, until lightly colored.*
8. *Press an upside-down chocolate kiss into the center of each hot cookie, and transfer to wire racks to cool.*

Refrigerator Spice Cookies

About 6 dozen

1/2 cup butter or margarine
1 cup packed dark brown sugar
1 large egg
1 teaspoon vanilla extract
2-1/4 cups all-purpose flour
1/2 teaspoon baking soda
1 teaspoon ground cinnamon
1/2 teaspoon ground nutmeg
1/4 teaspoon salt
1 cup finely chopped nuts
Oil or shortening, for greasing the cookie sheets

1. *In a bowl, using an electric mixer, beat together the butter and sugar until fluffy. Beat in the egg and vanilla.*
2. *In a second bowl, combine the flour, baking soda, cinnamon, nutmeg, and salt. Using your hands or a wooden spoon, work the dry ingredients into the butter mixture to form a soft dough. Work in the nuts and shape dough into a 2- to 2-1/2- inch log. Wrap in waxed paper and refrigerate for 24 hours, or until chilled solid.*
3. *Remove from the refrigerator, unwrap, and set aside for about 30 minutes.*
4. *Meanwhile, position a rack in the center of the oven and preheat to 350° F. Lightly grease cookie sheets.*
5. *Using a sharp knife, cut the log into thin slices 1/2- to 3/4-inch thick, and arrange on the prepared cookie sheets about 1-1/2 to 2 inches apart.*
6. *Bake for about 8 to 10 minutes, or until the edges start to turn golden. Remove from the oven and transfer to a wire rack to cool.*

Cookout Coolers

Garden Cocktail Party

SIPS AND STARTERS

•

Grandma's Ginger Ale Punch

Apple-Raspberry Punch

Baked Olive Bundles

Savory Stuffed Mushrooms

SALADS

•

Spinach Salad with Sherry-Cumin Vinaigrette

ENTREES

•

Golden Chicken

Grilled Prosciutto-Wrapped Sea Scallops

SIDES

•

Sautéed Zucchini with Tomatoes & Herbs

Herbed Orange Rice

FROM THE BAKERY

•

Cinnamon Coffee Cake

Banana Boat Cooler

8 to 10 servings

1 cup Creme de Banana
2 cups unsweetened pineapple juice
4 cups ginger ale, well chilled
Sliced banana, for garnish

Place ice cubes in a 2-quart serving pitcher, add the Creme de Banana, pineapple juice, and ginger ale. Add the banana slices and serve.

Cranberry Quencher

10 to 12 servings

2 jasmine tea bags
1 quart boiling water
1 (6 ounce) can frozen lemonade concentrate
1 quart cranberry juice cocktail
1 cup gin or vodka
1 lemon, thinly sliced, for garnish

In a saucepan or teapot, combine the teabags and water. Cover and set aside for at least 30 minutes. When ready, pour into a punch bowl or serving pitcher, add the lemonade, cranberry juice, and gin. Pour into cups or glasses of choice and garnish with lemon slices.

Apple-Raspberry Punch

6 to 8 servings

1 cup raspberry-flavored brandy
1 cup unsweetened apple cider
4 cups lemon-lime soda, chilled
Fresh raspberries, for garnish

Place ice cubes in a 2-quart serving pitcher, add the brandy, cider, and soda. Add the raspberries, and serve.

Fruity Fruit Cup Punch

About 6 to 8 servings

1 cup peach-flavored brandy

1/4 cup Triple Sec liqueur

4 cups club soda, well chilled

Sliced peaches and oranges, for garnish

Place ice cubes in a serving pitcher and add the brandy, liqueur, and soda. Garnish with the fruit of your choice and serve.

Apple Annie Fruit Punch

20 servings

1 liter apple brandy

3 ounces raspberry liqueur

1-1/2 cups orange juice (preferably freshly squeezed)

1 cup grapefruit juice (preferably freshly squeezed)

2 ounces lemon juice

1 orange, thinly sliced

1 lemon, thinly sliced

1 apple, cored and thinly sliced

1 liter ginger ale

1 liter club soda or lemon-lime soda

Combine the apple brandy, raspberry liqueur, and fruit juices in a large bowl and stir well. Add a large block of ice and garnish with the fruit slices. Add the sodas just before serving.

Champagne Sorbet Punch

About 20 to 25 servings

2 (750 milliliter) bottles Champagne or sparkling wine

1 (750 milliliter) bottle white dessert wine

1 quart lemon sorbet

Combine the Champagne and wine in a punch bowl with a block of ice and stir gently. Just before serving add another block of ice, and scoops of the lemon sorbet.

Sangria Punch

About 6 to 8 servings

1/2 cup fresh lemon juice, chilled
1/2 cup fresh orange juice, chilled
1/2 cup granulated sugar
3-1/4 cups dry red wine, chilled
1/4 cup brandy or rum
1 cup club soda, well chilled
1 cup sliced oranges
1 cup sliced apples
1 cup sliced peaches
Ice cubes or large block of ice

1. *In a large serving pitcher, blend together the lemon juice, orange juice, and sugar, stirring until the sugar is dissolved. Add the wine, brandy, and club soda.*
2. *In a bowl, combine the sliced fruits. Pour the punch mixture over the top, and serve.*

Wine Cooler

4 to 6 drinks

1/2 cup peach-flavored liqueur
1 large orange, sliced
1 bottle chilled Riesling or other Rhine wine
Mint sprigs, for garnish

Place ice cubes in a 1-quart serving pitcher, add the liqueur, orange slices, and wine. Pour into serving glasses, garnish with a sprig of mint, and serve.

Burgundy Punch

10 to 12 servings

1 cup orange peel, cut into matchsticks
1 cup boiling water
2 bottles Burgundy wine
1 cup orange curaçao liqueur
Orange wedges, for garnish

1. *In a saucepan, combine the orange peel and water. Set aside for about 15 minutes.*
2. *When ready, add the wine, and the liqueur. Heat through, without boiling, and serve in mugs, with orange wedges as a garnish.*

Beyond Beer: A Well-Stocked Bar

A well-stocked bar is the staple of anyone who entertains guests on a regular and frequent basis. But, as every-one knows, entertainment has its price, and a mountain of merchandise is required for a full-functioning bar. Still, plenty of delicious drinks can be made on a non-bank-breaking budget. A bartender's guide will help you make the drinks, but in the meantime, this basic checklist will get you going:

- BAR EQUIPMENT: *barspoon; blender; bottle opener (also known fondly as a "church key"); Champagne stopper; citrus spout; citrus stripper or vegetable peeler; corkscrew; juicer; ice crusher; shaker (standard and Boston); strainer; cutting board; knives; measuring cups; spoons*

- SPIRITS: *bourbon; brandy; cognac; gin; various liqueurs; light and dark rum; Scotch; tequila; sweet and dry vermouth; vodka; whiskey; wine; and a good selection of domestic and imported beer*

- MIXERS: *citrus juices; club soda; coconut milk; cola; cream; ginger ale; lemon-lime soda; tomato juice; water*

- FLAVORINGS: *bitters; grenadine; salt; sugar; Tabasco Sauce; Worcestershire sauce*

- GARNISHES: *celery; cinnamon sticks; cucumber spears; lemons; limes; maraschino cherries; mint; nutmeg; olives; oranges; pineapple; coarse salt; strawberries*

- SOME TIPS: *pre-chill proper glasses; use rock-solid ice, so drinks won't get watery; always use fresh juice and club soda; measure carefully. When stocking up on spirits, keep in mind mixers for those festive favorites like the margarita, gin and tonic, martini, rum and Coke, Tom Collins, and Bloody Mary.*

"Hooch," the slang term for whiskey, comes from "Hoochinoo," a powerful spirit distilled by the Chinook Indians.

Bloody Mary

About 8 servings

4-1/2 cups tomato juice
1 cup vodka
2 teaspoons prepared horseradish
2 teaspoons Worcestershire sauce
Salt and pepper, to taste
Bottled hot sauce, to taste
2 limes, quartered, for garnish

In a blender, combine the tomato juice, vodka, horseradish, Worcestershire sauce, salt and pepper to taste, and hot sauce to taste. Process on high for about 2 minutes. Pour into chilled serving glasses, garnish with a piece of lime, and serve.

Chocolate Shakes

4 to 6 servings

4 cups milk
1 package chocolate pudding mix
1 tablespoon crème de cacao or amaretto liqueur
Ice cubes (optional)
Mint sprigs, for garnish

In a blender, combine the milk, pudding mix, and crème de cacao. Process on high until smooth. Add the ice cubes, process until blended, pour into serving glasses, and serve with a sprig of mint for garnish.

Minted Ginger Tea

6 to 8 servings

1-3/4 cups white crème de menthe
1 cup cold brewed tea
1-1/2 cups ginger ale, well chilled
Mint sprigs, for garnish

Place ice cubes in a 2-quart serving pitcher and add the crème de menthe, tea, and ginger ale. Pour into well chilled serving glasses, add a mint sprig, and serve.

Coffee Toddy

About 4 servings

3 tablespoons instant espresso coffee granules
1 teaspoon pumpkin pie spice
3 tablespoons granulated sugar
2 cups milk
1 teaspoon almond extract, or 1 tablespoon amaretto liqueur
1/4 cup brandy or rum

In a saucepan, combine the coffee, pumpkin pie spice, sugar, milk, and almond extract. Heat, stirring until the sugar is dissolved, and bubbles form around the edge of the pan. Remove from the heat, stir in the brandy, and serve.

Bubbly Punch

10 servings

2 quarts white grape juice
2 liters diet lemon-lime soda
1 liter club soda

1. *Place all of the bottles in the coldest part of the refrigerator, and chill for at least 4 hours before needed.*
2. *When ready, in a larger serving bowl, combine all of the chilled liquids, pour over ice cubes, and serve.*

Fruit Bowl

4 to 6 servings

1-1/4 cups fresh orange juice
1 cup peeled, seeded, diced watermelon
1/2 cup fresh raspberries, rinsed and patted dry
1/2 cup fresh strawberries, rinsed and patted dry
1/2 cup canned diced pineapple, drained
1/4 cup unsweetened applesauce
1 kiwi fruit, peeled and sliced
1 small fresh pear, cored, peeled, and sliced

In a blender or food processor, combine the juice and assortment of fruits, and process on high until smooth. Cover tightly and chill in the refrigerator for at least 6 hours before serving.

Honey Lemonade

8 to 10 servings

1 cup honey, warm
1 cup hot water
3/4 cup lemon juice concentrate
8 cups cold water

In a saucepan combine the honey and hot water. Heat through, but do not boil. Remove from the heat, cool slightly, and stir in the lemon juice and cold water. Chill in the refrigerator for at least 2 hours, and pour into chilled glasses filled with ice.

Mango Mambo

About 4 servings

2 cups mango purée

2 cups crushed ice

1/2 cup coconut cream (not coconut milk)

Sliced mango, for garnish

In a blender, combine the mango purée, ice, coconut cream, and process on high until just blended. Serve in chilled glasses and garnish with mango slices.

Rhubarb Punch

4 to 6 servings

2 pounds fresh rhubarb, peeled and chopped

4 cups water

3/4 cup granulated sugar

5 teaspoons fresh squeezed orange juice

1 tablespoon fresh lemon juice

3/4 cup club soda

1. *In a saucepan, combine the rhubarb and water, bring to a boil, reduce to a simmer, cover and cook for about 15 minutes. Remove from the heat and cool slightly.*
2. *When ready, strain through a fine nylon sieve, or a triple thickness of cheesecloth. Set aside to drain for several hours.*
3. *When ready, discard the rhubarb pulp, and add the sugar, orange juice, and lemon juice, stirring until the sugar is dissolved. Pour into a serving pitcher, and add the club soda. Serve at once in chilled serving glasses.*

Dad's Homemade Ginger Ale

4 to 6 servings

2 tablespoons grated fresh ginger root

2 tablespoons grated lemon zest

1/4 cup warm honey, or to taste

1 cup water

1 quart club soda

In a saucepan, combine the ginger root, lemon zest, honey, and water. Bring to a boil, cover tightly, and remove from the heat. Add the club soda and set aside, undisturbed, for at least 1 hour. Strain before serving.

Grandma's Ginger Ale Punch

About 4 quarts

1 quart cranberry juice, chilled

1 quart lemonade, chilled

1 quart pineapple juice, chilled

1 quart ginger ale, chilled

Chilled lemon-lime soda, to taste

In a large bowl, combine the cranberry juice, lemonade, pineapple juice, and ginger ale. Add lemon-lime soda to taste, making sure not to dilute the flavor too much. Serve at once in tall glasses over ice.

Dream a Little Theme

THEORY: A little imagination and preparation can go a long way
PROOF OF THEORY: Theme Party

A theme party can be a fun alternative to an otherwise humdrum social event. With the help of a theme, everyone can step a little out of character and right into party mode.

For a Hawaiian luau, deck the yard with outdoor torches and slap some palm fronds and bamboo onto the porch. Visit a party supply store to pick up some leis for greeting your guests, and miniature umbrellas to adorn their tropical beverage treats. Then stop at a music store for a selection of Hawaiian island music, usually found in the international section of major stores. Make sure your guests know they're expected to don the requisite flower-print shirts. At the end of the evening, step back for a moment to watch the crowd swaying to the lulling sounds of a lazy slide guitar and a ukulele in your self-made tropical paradise.

Everyone loves Mardi Gras, but not all of us are fortunate enough to visit New Orleans for the festivities. Bring the fun to your friends with a well-planned, at-home Mardi Gras celebration. Masks, party favors, beads, a good mix of Dixieland, Cajun, and jazz music, and a lot of bourbon should do the trick.

Miss the days of old? Any genre can be re-created. Try the late 1960s or early '70s as your theme. Dust off the old Jefferson Airplane records, fire up some incense, turn the lava lamp on, and let your bellbottom-wearing friends dig the groovy scene.

Banana Strawberry Freeze

2 servings

1 banana, frozen and sliced
4 ounces frozen strawberries
White grape juice

Combine the banana and strawberries in a blender. Blend at lowest speed, slowly adding the grape juice through the top of the blender until creamy and frothy. Pour into chilled glasses and serve.

Bee's Kiss

2 servings

10 ounces fresh orange juice
2 scoops vanilla frozen yogurt
1 teaspoon honey
1/2 teaspoon vanilla extract

Combine the orange juice, frozen yogurt, honey, and vanilla extract in a blender and blend until smooth. Pour into chilled glasses and serve.

Charlie's Angel

2 servings

10 ounces pineapple juice
4 ounces grapefruit juice
8 fresh strawberries, hulled and sliced
2 bananas, peeled and sliced
2 whole strawberries, for garnish

Combine all ingredients except the whole strawberries in a blender and blend until smooth. If the mixture is too thick, add more pineapple or grapefruit juice until desired consistency is achieved. Pour into chilled glasses, garnish each with a whole strawberry, and serve.

Klondike Annie

2 servings

5 ounces coconut milk
5 ounces pineapple juice
2 pineapple wedges, for garnish

Combine liquid ingredients with cracked ice in a blender and blend until slushy. Pour into chilled glasses, garnish with the pineapple wedges, and serve.

Simple Smoothies in a Snap

Sorry, snowcone. Apologies, popsicle. There is no better summertime treat than a good smoothie. Period. These refreshing and delicious fruit drinks are not only healthy, they're simple to make. All you need is a blender and a few choice ingredients to make your best beverage. Smoothies usually start from a base of liquid—orange juice, apple juice, pineapple juice, even milk. Then just toss in the fruit ingredients. Bananas, strawberries, peaches, apples—all offer the makings of a great smoothie. Fresh fruit is best for flavor, but frozen works well, too, and can make a frothier treat. A few ice cubes will also furnish froth. Some folks add vanilla extract to sweeten the deal. Although they can be frozen, smoothies are generally best fresh out of the blender.

There are a million recipes for and ideas about making the best smoothie, which means only that tastes vary—everything is relative, so experiment. Go heavy on bananas once; ease off next time. Try new ingredients. Try different combinations. Have fun . . . it's healthy. So next time junior opens the fridge to grab a soda, offer a smoothie; and consider slipping a carrot into the blender when he's not looking.

Lemon Blueberry Freeze

2 servings

8 ounces blueberries
4 scoops lemon sorbet
White grape juice

Combine the berries and sorbet in a blender. Blend at the lowest speed, slowly adding grape juice through the top of the blender until desired consistency is achieved. Pour into chilled highball glasses and serve.

Great Games for your Garden Soiree

Some time-honored outdoor games can lend an air of refinement to your garden party.

- BADMINTON: *Serve the birdie over the net and let fly. A combination of tennis and volleyball, this lawn game is played with lightweight rackets and a shuttlecock. The shuttlecock is also known as a "birdie," perhaps because it was historically made by fastening 16 goose feathers to a small cork.*

- CROQUET: *Knock balls through hoops in what seems like an older variation of miniature golf. The game is played on a smooth lawn with long-handled mallets that the players use to hit billiard-sized balls through wickets. An earlier version called "paille-maille" was enjoyed in 13th-century France.*

- BOCCE: *Also spelled "bocci," this Italian bowling game is played on an 8-foot-wide court that stretches approximately 75 feet in length. Of course, any decent stretch of flat grass or dirt will do. Genoa, Italy, hosted the first bocce world championships in 1951.*

Honey Apple Tea

6 to 8 servings

4 black tea bags
3 cups boiling water
1/3 cup honey, warm
3 cups unsweetened apple juice
1 lemon, thickly sliced

In a saucepan, cover the tea bags with the boiling water and allow to steep for about 2 to 3 minutes. Remove the tea bags, add the honey and apple juice, and pour into cups. Garnish with lemon slices, and serve.

Kai's Ginger Tea

2 to 3 cups

2 to 3 cups water
1/2 cup packed light brown sugar
1 piece (about 3 inches) ginger root, peeled and chopped

1. In a saucepan, combine the water, sugar, and ginger root. Bring to a boil, cover tightly and continue to brew for about 2 minutes. Remove from heat (do not remove the cover), and set aside for about 2 to 3 minutes.
2. When ready, pour into cups, and serve.

Mulled Cider

4 to 6 servings

1 quart sweetened apple cider
10 whole cloves
1/4 cup granulated sugar
6 cinnamon sticks
7 whole allspice

1. In a saucepan, combine the cider, cloves, sugar, cinnamon, and allspice. Bring to a boil, reduce to a simmer, and cook for about 15 minutes. Remove from the heat and set aside, undisturbed, for about 12 hours.
2. When ready, strain through a fine sieve, reheat, and serve.

This can also be made with hard cider.

Sinless Sangria

6 servings

4 cups red grape juice

1 cup orange juice (preferably freshly squeezed)

1/2 cup fresh lemon juice

1/2 cup honey

1 tablespoon orange zest

1 tablespoon lemon zest

1 teaspoon almond extract

1/2 teaspoon allspice

1/2 teaspoon nutmeg

5 cinnamon sticks

10 whole cloves

Orange slices, for garnish

In a large stockpot, combine all of the ingredients except the orange slices over low heat for at least 1 hour. Serve hot in warm mugs garnished with the orange slices.

Hot to Trot

6 servings

3 cups carrot juice

2-1/2 cups orange juice (preferably freshly squeezed)

About 15–20 dashes Tabasco Sauce, to taste

Celery sticks, for garnish

In a large pitcher over cracked ice, combine all the ingredients except the celery sticks. Pour into chilled glasses, garnish with the celery sticks, and serve.

Tomato Juice Cocktail

8 to 10 servings

1 (48 ounce) can tomato juice

3 tablespoons fresh lime juice

2 teaspoons salt

1/8 to 1/4 teaspoon bottled hot sauce

2 teaspoons ground cumin

Celery sticks, for garnish

In a blender, combine 1 cup of the tomato juice with the lime juice, salt, hot sauce, and cumin. Process on low until smooth. Add the remaining tomato juice, pour into a pitcher, or chilled glasses, garnish with the celery sticks, and serve.

Energy Drink

4 to 6 servings

6 large carrots, pared and diced

4 sticks celery, chopped

1 piece (4 inches) ginger root, peeled and chopped

2 tablespoons apple juice

2 drops bottled hot sauce

1 tablespoon fresh lemon juice

1. *In a blender, combine the carrots, celery, ginger, and apple juice and process on high until smooth. Cover the blender container and chill in the refrigerator until needed.*
2. *When ready, add the hot sauce and lemon juice, and process on high to blend. Pour into chilled glasses and serve.*

Get to Know Your Grill

As humankind has evolved, so too has the art of grilling. So many now are the techniques and methods employed, there are not enough pages in the most voluminous of tomes to explain it all. But briefly, the Cliffs Notes version, broken into two general parts: charcoal-fired grills and gas grills.

- CHARCOAL-FIRED: Charcoal-fired grills are undeniably messier than their gas grill cousins, but many people feel they retain more of the natural flavor that may be lost with the gas grill. Of the charcoal grills, there are those that are open and those that are closed. The hibachi, for example, is a small open grill that sits low to the ground. Though limited in size and temperature control, hibachis are efficient for transporting and grilling small items such as burgers or chicken breasts. Although less mobile, a larger open grill offers more room to shift food around between hotter and cooler sections of the grill. Covered grills, on the other hand, can cook food by direct heat, which is diffused by the dome cover and adjusted by controlling the flow of air through vents in the cover. Also, these grills can cook certain foods more efficiently, such as whole turkeys and roasts.

- CHARCOAL-GRILL FUELS: Lump charcoal, made from hardwoods (mesquite, alder, and hickory) or fruit woods (such as cherry and peach), burns slowly and hot, but does not cook as evenly as briquettes; briquettes are easy, safe and convenient—they travel well and they're less messy than lump charcoal. However, they contain binders and, occasionally, sodium nitrite to speed ignition, which, it is hoped, will burn off during cooking. Even more convenient—and more expensive—than standard briquettes are instant-lighting briquettes, which are infused with fuel; electric starters, characterized by metal loops submerged in the charcoal, require outlets and the heating elements can be damaged if left in the fire too long; lighter fluid typically adds chemical flavors, especially when used excessively; other starter aids include paraffin blocks and wax-coated wood chips.

- GAS GRILLS: More popular—cleaner and quicker too—are gas grills. If you're in the market for a new one, try to get one with a durable cast-iron or brass burner.

- FUEL/HEATING ELEMENTS FOR GAS GRILLS: Propane is widely

available and fuel gauges can be attached to the tanks to alert you of the fuel level. The primary heating elements in gas grills are lava rocks,  metal rods, and ceramic briquettes. Lava rocks are ideal in that they absorb the juices of the food to produce more flavorful smoke during grilling, and there's no need to replace them. Metal rods provide even heat distribution but cause more flare-ups. Ceramic briquettes provide even heat distribution and are less susceptible to flare-ups.

Some General Grilling Rules & Tips:

- Spread a single layer of briquettes wide enough to extend one inch beyond the food surface. If grilling for an extended period, a double layer of briquettes may be a good strategy. After igniting, wait until the outside of the charcoal develops a fine layer of gray ash before slapping the meat on.

- For strategic grilling, mound some briquettes in one area of the grill for intense heat while placing just a single layer elsewhere for lower heat.

- To test the heat level, hold your hand about six inches above the cooking surface. If you can hold it there for more than six seconds, you have a low fire; five seconds, a medium fire; less than three seconds, a hot fire.

- Plan on waiting at least 30 minutes after the charcoal is lit before slapping food on the grill. Gas grills should be preheated for about 15 minutes.

- Food should be at room temperature before it hits the heat, so let it sit out of the fridge for about 30 minutes.

- There are numerous excellent guides and reference materials that will help you along in crafting your grill skills.

Grilling Tools and Other Essentials

Grilling tools are of utmost importance. They are to the backyard griller what the stethoscope is to the doctor, or the siren to the ambulance. Without these implements, the difficulty of each goal will multiply tenfold. The doctor will misdiagnose the patient; the ambulance will get stuck in traffic; and saddest of all, the food will be left in the hands of a defenseless grill guardian!

Again, it is recommended that you take some time to know your grill. This intimacy will help determine the accessories you really need. Among a multitude of possible essentials, consider the following:

- Long-handled tongs, spatulas, and brushes. Tongs release less vital juice than forks; spatulas are good for burgers and chicken breasts, and wider ones work particularly well for whole fish; brushes are indispensable for applying sauces or marinades.

- Enamel-covered grill tops with small holes that fit over grill grates can prevent small items such as shrimp or scallops from falling into the inferno below.

- A non-stick or stick-resistant fish basket can hold various sizes of fish tightly, plus vegetables, and even burgers—those items that threaten to break apart when you try to remove them with a spatula.

- Long metal skewers, with rings or other graspable handles, for kebabs.

- Instant-read thermometers help with large pieces of meat.

Different Heats for Different Meats

Although your grill, like a car, may have its own character and eccentricities that take a little time to appreciate, here are some general guidelines for cooking meat over an open flame.

- CHICKEN: Chicken should be turned over frequently to get it cooked evenly without searing the skin. For whole chickens, 40 minutes over a medium flame should suffice, but be sure to turn it every 10 minutes. If you're adding a barbecue sauce, do so after 30 minutes, or 10 minutes before you anticipate the chicken to be ready. Test for doneness by cutting into a thick piece—there should be no pink meat and juices should run clear. For chicken breasts cooked over a medium flame, times may vary between 6 and 12 minutes. So remain conscientious of the time or your chicken may dry out faster than that load of laundry.

- BEEF: Throw the flame on high and oil up the grates. Steak is easy but patience and timing are prerequisites. Trim strips of fat that are more than a 1/4-inch thick and, after washing the steak, season as desired. After the grill has been preheated, slap the meat on and close the lid, if you have a lid. Turn the steak over after 1 minute. Repeat after another minute. Approximate the width of your steak (1-inch, 1-1/2-inches, 2-inches) and grill for another 2 minutes plus 1 minute for each 1/2-inch. Then turn and repeat for the same time on the flip side. Check for doneness with a meat thermometer—if you've got one. (140° F for rare, 150° F for medium rare, 160° F for medium, 165° F for medium well, burnt for well done.) Let steak rest and its juices pool for a couple of minutes, and then dig in. (The same temperature rules apply to burgers as well.)

- PORK: In days of old, less-than-well-done pork made people wary. These days, however, the little trichinosis bacteria we feared are pretty rare, and pork should be cooked the way it was intended—till slightly pink and still juicy (cooking it to an internal temperature of more than 160° F results in dry, rubbery meat). One- to 1-1/2-inch thick chops should be grilled directly over high heat for about 8 to 12 minutes, and a tenderloin should be cooked indirectly over high heat for about 12 to 16 minutes

- LAMB: For the best flavor, lamb should usually be cooked to medium rare or medium. Tougher cuts of lamb, like shoulder chops, should be marinated first to tenderize the meat. Other cuts, like loin chops, cubes, and patties, can go straight on the grill without marinating (though a marinade always adds some zing). Lamb shoulder chops should be cooked for 9 to 12 minutes for medium rare, 12 to 14 minutes for medium. Loin chops and cubes should be cooked for 7 to 9 minutes or 9 to 11 minutes, depending on desired doneness. And patties, which cook more quickly, should be grilled for 3 to 5 or 5 to 7 minutes.

- FISH: It depends on what kind of fish you have, but basting—with something as simple as lemon and butter—should be done for all. Flaky fish should generally be laid on a piece of heavy aluminum foil over the grill, or else grilled in a basket, so pieces will not fall through. Larger fish should be brushed inside and out with olive oil or melted butter. Try stuffing onion slivers and fresh herbs into the fish for flavor. Seal the fish in heavy aluminum foil and, depending on size, grill for 6 to 8 minutes on each side. The challenge of grilling fish is knowing when your fish is done. Look for meat that flakes easily with a fork and appears opaque all the way through. If any part is glossy, keep on grillin'.